EIGHTEEN YEARS ON
THE GOLD COAST OF AFRICA

EIGHTEEN YEARS

ON

THE GOLD COAST
OF AFRICA

including an account of the native tribes, and their
intercourse with Europeans

BRODIE CRUICKSHANK

With a new introduction by
K. A. BUSIA

VOLUME TWO

SECOND EDITION

FRANK CASS & CO. LTD.
1966

Published by Frank Cass & Co. Ltd.,
10 Woburn Walk, London W.C.1

First edition	1853
Second edition	1966

Printed in Great Britain
Thomas Nelson (Printers) Ltd., London and Edinburgh

EIGHTEEN YEARS

ON

THE GOLD COAST

OF AFRICA.

INCLUDING AN ACCOUNT OF THE NATIVE TRIBES, AND THEIR
INTERCOURSE WITH EUROPEANS.

BY

BRODIE CRUICKSHANK,

MEMBER OF THE LEGISLATIVE COUNCIL, CAPE COAST CASTLE.

IN TWO VOLUMES.
VOL. II.

LONDON:
HURST AND BLACKETT, PUBLISHERS,
SUCCESSORS TO HENRY COLBURN,
13, GREAT MARLBOROUGH STREET.
1853.

CONTENTS

CHAPTER IV.

CHAPTER V.

CHAPTER VI.

CHAPTER VII.

CHAPTER VIII.

CHAPTER IX.

CHAPTER X.

CHAPTER XI.

EIGHTEEN YEARS

ON

THE GOLD COAST.

CHAPTER I.

The great degradation of the African owing to a constitutional law of our nature—Assertion of the natural
affections—The authority of the local government—Its
great moral power—Insubordination of Chiefs—Alarm of
the Fetishmen — Causes of our extensive influence—
Necessity for maintaining it—Diminished power of the
Chiefs—The Governor's necessary severity—Establishment of good order—Its effect upon men's minds—
Poverty of the people — More general union of the
members of a family—Frequent appeals made to the
Governor—A better understanding and full confidence
established—Caution in carrying out reforms — Great
influence of the decisions given in Court.

THE ordinary effect of misfortune upon mankind, when not under the influence of Christian
feeling is to beget a selfishness, dead alike to the
voice of nature and humanity.   We accordingly

find that the long series of miseries, which for ages pressed upon this unfortunate race, begat in them a brutish insensibility to human suffering. Occupied entirely with the care of their individual interests, and checked in their pursuit by no moral restraint, every imagination of the thoughts of the heart became their only rule of life, and the natural and inevitable consequence of this guidance was, of course, what unerring wisdom had declared it invariably to be, " only evil continually." To such depths of degradation had man's natural depravity conducted the African, that the natives of more favoured lands, in the pride of superior acquirements, have sometimes scorned to admit them to an equality of origin. This has not been a prejudice of the ignorant only, but many who considered themselves entitled to be regarded as philosophers, and as lights of the world, have written and argued in defence of this doctrine.

A little attention to the corrupt tendency of the human heart, and of the consequence of yielding to its dictates, in the total extinction of every seed of goodness, might, we think, have led the candid inquirer to see that the complete demoralization of the African is owing to a constitutional law of our nature, to which the white man and the black are equally subject. He might have learned, by a reference to the early records of the most favoured nations of the earth, that wherever gross ignorance and an idolatrous worship have prevailed, the work of corruption has been uninterrupted and progressive, and that the debasement and elevation of individual man, as well as of nations, have been in exact proportion to the moral standard of his worship. If he will admit this much, the long ages of dark superstition which has kept the African mind in thrall, and the influences of external and internal lawlessness and oppression, will, we think, sufficiently account for its moral debasement, without having recourse to any original inferiority of nature.

It has been the misfortune of this race to labour under a greater accumulation of miseries than has fallen to the lot of any other, and to have been continually subjected to them for a longer period. During these long ages of progressive debasement, the principle of evil in our nature became so strengthened and confirmed by habitual exercise, and the reasoning faculty so powerless, that the proneness of the African to evil assumed the character of an undeviating instinct, to which the absence of any sufficient legal restraint gave the utmost scope. But though thus fallen and ruined, without an apparent vestige of any higher destiny than their mean and grovelling desires and

pursuits indicated, there yet existed in their minds
—obscured and defaced, it is true, but still unextin-
guished—the glimmering of a purer ray, which
needed only a more genial atmosphere for its
brighter development. That this has been the
case, a review of the progress made during the last
twenty years will sufficiently prove.

As soon as the minds of men began to recover
from the deadly paralysis, which was the result
of the accumulation of evils that had so long
afflicted them, and to experience some relief from
the incessant blight which kept withering every
sickly bud of hope that sprung up in their breasts,
feelings of natural affection were the first to assert
their claim for redress.

Cheerless and desolate as the home of the
African had in general been, without those endearing associations which hallow it in the eyes of
more favoured nations, it nevertheless still formed
the load-star to which their thoughts, relieved
from the cares of self-preservation, became ultimately attached. Even many, to whom the
domestic affections had never been known, longing
for human sympathy, and feeling the aching void
of the heart, yearned to relieve their oppressed
feelings in the bosom of some one, whom they
could regard as connected with them by the ties of

blood. The dispersion of a brood of chickens, and the wide and sudden separation of a flock of sheep with their restless wanderings and plaintive cries to be re-united, form no inapt representations of the condition of the Gold Coast at the time to which we refer. But man's havoc among his fellow-men is more irreparable than that committed by the beasts of prey upon their quarry. A long series of years has not yet healed the wounds which were inflicted, and generations yet unborn will be affected by them. Much, however, has been done to alleviate their calamities.

The acknowledgment of the independence of the Fantees and other allied tribes, which the English government wrung from the Ashantees, relieved the country from its most oppressive load; and the consequent supervision of its general police by the government, affected such a salutary improvement in the increased facility and security of communication, that such redress as the peculiar circumstances of the social condition of the people admitted, was open to all. It must be remembered, that the fundamental constitution of society was neither affected by this independence, nor by the protectorate of England. The same servile dependence of families upon their head, of vassals on their lord, and of slaves on their master, which has been already described, continued to exist in full force. Now, as before, individuals were given in pawn, and sold into slavery, according to the necessities of their relations and owners. The individuals of a household had still a property value in the estimation of its head, and human beings still formed a portion of the currency of the country.

The great step gained was the limitation which the suppression of lawlessness put upon this system, and the opportunity which a good police and an impartial administration of justice afforded to every one, of resisting unjust claims for the present, and of obtaining relief from such as had been iniquitously established in time past.

Nothing could more forcibly demonstrate their need of a disinterested superior, and their estimation of the advantages derived from his superintending justice, than the fact, that with a corps of one hundred and twenty men, natives of the country, and with pecuniary resources not exceeding, annually, £4,000, Governor Maclean maintained for a series of years an undisputed sway over an immense extent of territory, comprising a numerous population, composed of different tribes, speaking different languages, and many of them possessed of great physical power.

There have been few instances in the history of the world of such an extensive influence, so completely the result of moral force. But it must not be imagined that it had the effect of entirely putting a stop to unjust practices, or of effecting any vital revolution in the principles upon which their general polity was grounded. The remembrance of their uncontrolled power was too fresh in the minds of the chiefs, and the temptation to relapse into their former tyranny too strong, to be always successfully resisted. The distance of many of them also from the seat of the controlling power was so great, and the detection of their mal-practices, on that account, so uncertain, that the restraint of fear did not always operate with the unvarying precision which was essential for the prevention of injustice. Exalted conceptions also of their physical power, of their kingly state, and of the traditionary glory of their ancestors, which the flattery of interested sycophants kept continually ringing in their ears, placed their submission to a superior in a degrading point of view, and induced them to make comparisons between their power and the physical strength of the government, favourable to their own consequence, and inconsistent with perfect obedience.

These considerations, coupled with the instinctive alarm of the priesthood, who intuitively perceived that the domination of the Europeans would greatly impair their influence, and who therefore used it, while it remained to them, to warn their countrymen against incurring the displeasure of the gods by a departure from the customs of their fathers, kept alive a refractory spirit, which occasionally manifested itself in acts of cruelty and oppression in open defiance of any superior authority. And as acts of obvious injustice could not always be prevented, so neither could any radical change be effected in the fundamental structure of society. The relative positions of its members had been the result of a progressive growth, which might well bear a nobler graft, productive of better fruit than that of the natural branch, but whose stem and roots could not be disturbed without endangering its vitality, and hastening its decay.

But although it was found impossible to prevent injustice at all times, yet redress of injuries was generally within the power of the government, nothwithstanding the temporary obstructions and delays which were inseparable from the very nature of its influence. Had it been based on physical force, injustice would have been less frequent, and its redress and punishment more consequent on its commission; but it is doubtful whether the effect in gradually moulding the inclinations of the people, and in diffusing generally a more humane spirit, would have been so salutary and lasting by the resistless opposition of superior force, as by the exhibition of an undeviating course of justice, struggling with difficulties, often baffled, but never dismayed, and persevering with an untiring firmness to the accomplishment of its object.

In the one case, the impression left on the mind is merely what they had seen exhibited among themselves—the coercion of the weak by the strong; in the other, they have leisure to contemplate the moral government of the world, to trace effects through all their intricate windings to their original cause, to observe the certainty of punishment following a deviation from rectitude and justice, and to arrive at the wise conclusion that " honesty is the best policy."

We would not, by these remarks, be understood to undervalue the importance of a sufficient coercive force. On the contrary, to ensure good government, there ought to be present in the minds of the governed the conviction that the government can at all times, when necessity requires it, bring a physical force to bear more than sufficient to crush every opposition. There is no necessity for continually parading this force. Indeed, it is not necessary even that it should be known whence, on any occasion of emergency, it is to spring up. It is sufficient that the executive should be surrounded by such symbols of his authority, as will protect him from insult, ensure respect, and enable him to provide for the ordinary administration of justice. When extraordinary emergencies occur, the moral influence of the government will become the source of its physical force, and will raise defenders sufficient to quell the disaffected, and to enforce justice.

The peculiar circumstances of our position on the Gold Coast have hitherto rendered a large military force unnecessary. The very important part which we played in the war which led to their independence, and the indication of the exhaustless nature of our pecuniary resources, apparent in the great recklessness of expense during the progress of the war; the necessity of a protector against the power and ambition of the Ashantees, and their own inability to maintain their independence; the mutual fear and jealousy of rival chiefs, which made a common superior necessary to prevent discord; the tyranny of chiefs over their dependants, and of masters over their slaves; and a general belief in the rectitude of our intentions, and the impartiality of our justice; all conspired to influence the minds of every class, to elevate us into power, and to make common cause in maintaining our authority.

This power once assumed, the necessity of maintaining it with a firm hand against encroachments from without, and feuds, discords, and disobedience from within, involved the existence of the settlements, and the very principle of self-preservation. The causes of an occasional refractory spirit have been briefly adverted to. The supervision of the government tended to lessen the consequence of the chiefs, to curtail the sources of their emolument by the prevention of indiscriminate extortion and injustice, to elevate the condition of their dependants, and to obtain for them a consideration to which, until then, they had been utter strangers. The impartiality of our decisions, the equal distribution of justice to rich and to poor, the curb put upon the oppressor, and the general trammels which sought to tame down the restive and almost incorrigible tempers of the chiefs to a proper degree of submissive obedience, made them sigh for a return of former lawlessness, and almost regret that they had thrown off the yoke of the King of Ashantee, who, provided he obtained his revenue, did not care how much his vassal chiefs oppressed their people.

Under the influence of this discontented spirit, individual chiefs have, upon several occasions, attempted to assert their independence, and to resist the authority of the government; but although a partial and temporary success has sometimes attended their efforts, yet they have never been able to withstand its power for any length of time. The arms of rebellion have dropped one by one from their hands, without the intervention of force, and left them naked and defenceless, at the mercy of the government. Their own dependants, sensible of their increased privileges through the intervention of the Europeans, did not desire to see their chiefs independent of control, and were therefore lukewarm in their support. Rival chiefs could not endure that one of their number should presume to withdraw himself from a control to which they were subject, and joined heart and hand in enforcing submission. The freedom of communication and our relations with Ashantee rendered the independence of a single chief inconsistent with the general peace of the country. The cries of obstructed justice, which roused a spirit of retaliation, obliged the governor to cut off the rebellious from any external communication, and to shut them up in their own country; and if need was, and nothing else would counsel submission, a demonstration of brute force still remained to overpower all opposition.

Such an overwhelming amount of influence might be supposed sufficient to eradicate every seed of disobedience from the heart, and to render a repetition of the same offence incredible ; but neither the hopelessness of the attempt, the certainty of punishment, motives of self-interest, nor the perfect conviction in the minds of the offenders themselves, in their moments of sober reflection, of the utility and absolute necessity of European control, could restrain the wild bursts of passion to which the ungovernable mind of man in his natural state is subject, nor check his inherent tendency to transgress, and to harden himself in his transgressions. The consequence of this seemingly irreclaimable disposition made the intercourse between the governor and the chiefs, especially at the outset, a continual series of offences on the part of the latter, and of punishment, of pardon, and of re-instatement to his favour, on the part of the former.

The frequency of these contumacious delinquencies, and the necessity for severity, gave to the government the character of extreme harshness, and for some years occasioned an incessant struggle between the governor and the chiefs, who could ill brook to submit themselves to regular rules of conduct. Fines after fines were imposed with startling rapidity ; restitution to the uttermost farthing was rigidly enforced in every case of wrong ; even imprisonment and deposition were powerless in establishing a confirmed habit of obedience. The happy contrivance of giving pledges for their peaceable behaviour was at last had recourse to, and in a short time there was not a chief of any consequence in the country who had not been compelled to lodge in Cape Coast Castle the greater part of his property in gold, as security for his general good conduct, and for his appearance before the governor at any time that he might be summoned to answer a complaint against him.

To such an extent was this thoughtlessness and disregard of consequences carried, and such was their want of self-control, that even in the town of Cape Coast, under the walls of the castle, and in the presence of the governor and his whole garrison, it was necessary to have recourse to the same system, and to take security of the elders for the orderly behaviour of the inhabitants. And now we had a most gratifying corroboration of the truth of that text in Scripture which declares, that " where our treasure is, there will our heart be also ;" for no sooner was the treasure of the chiefs lodged in the strong box of the castle, than their devotion to the governor, and obedience to his commands, became the rule of their life. These deposits were returnable to their owners after a certain period of probation, and were renewed or given up according to the character which each individual chief had managed to establish for himself; and as a proof that they answered the end intended, there are, out of a very numerous list, only on record a few instances of forfeiture.

By this simple expedient, and the posting of a soldier in the principal towns of the different districts, to maintain an open communication throughout the country, to report misdemeanors to the governor, to signify his wishes to the chiefs with whom they resided, to assist them in maintaining their authority over their people, and generally to keep all in mind of the duty of obedience, good order and tranquillity were completely established.

From this time we are to date a new era in the history of the Gold Coast. Never, until now, had there been any scope afforded for the development of the better qualities of our nature. The liberty accorded was still prescribed, but a dreadful incubus had been removed, and men began to breathe more freely, and to become conscious of feelings and of rights of which they had previously no conception. We are now to see whether there is not something in the African which, under the influence of favourable circumstances, entertains as readily and as eagerly responds to good impressions as in the European; and to enable us to draw the parallel with greater justice, we must carry back our historical recollections to the worst days of European serfdom and superstition, and compare the slow process by which the fetters which enslaved both the body and the mind were shaken off, with the account which we are to give of the initiative taken in this country.

No sooner was it fully apparent that protection was afforded to every one, than a new spirit seemed to pervade the general mass of the people. It was like the awakening from a dream which had dissipated the senses, and left no tangible impression upon the mind, and required a process of careful reflection to arrive at a proper comprehension of their position. It was a boon which was regarded by many with mixed feelings of grief and joy—of hope and fear. To some it had come too late: the spoiler had already seized his prey, and left none of a numerous family to sympathise with their feelings; and to such the contemplation of another's joy was only the renewal of their grief.

Others rejoiced in the prospect of peaceful days, in which they might sit at ease under their own palms in the undisturbed enjoyment of the society of their friends and relations; many clung to the hope of being able to reunite the scattered numbers of their several families, and devoted themselves to a diligent search after them, with the view of endeavouring to redeem them from the bondage in which they were held; while others set about this anxious labour in doubt and fear, without a trace of the lost ones, and ignorant in which direction to turn their steps.

So general an emotion on the part of a people, expressed in such an unequivocal manner as soon as the most distant prospect of relief was opened up to them, is a sufficient indication, at least, that there was no want of natural affection; and that though misery may have deadened those feelings, or circumstances may have rendered the exhibition of them worse than useless, yet they had never been extinguished.

How often may the calmness of despair have been mistaken for insensibility, and the perfect inutility of any exhibition of grief for a callous indifference! It would have been happy for this people, if the gratification of those feelings had been as much within their reach as within their inclination; but years have been passed by many in a fruitless search; others have been discovered in the chains of an incurable bondage; some have been traced to the cane-fields of Cuba and Brazil; and not a few have poured forth their blood to grace a heathen holiday, or to gild the tombs of the Kings of Ashantee. Undismayed, however, by difficulties, and persevering in spite of disappointment, the main object of the general body of the population for the last twenty years has been for each to raise the broken walls of his family house, and to gather his widely-scattered relatives under the shadow of its roof.

But, independently of the impossibility of success in such contingencies as we have alluded to, the difficulties were by no means easily overcome, even where the residence and circumstances of the different members of a family were known. It will be remembered that we have represented society on the Gold Coast as being composed, with sundry modifications, of only the two classes—of master and slave; that property in slaves is considered the most valuable of all kinds of possessions; and that the constitution of society had not been affected by the protectorate of England. Bearing this in mind, as well as the processes by which the work of enslaving was carried on—namely, by a money value, or by assistance and protection considered equivalent to a purchase, it will be seen that more was necessary than the mere discovery of the residence of a relation to be united to him. He was the property of a master, from whom he had to be redeemed before he could cast off his yoke—of a master perhaps, who, if he had bought him formally, might refuse a redemption price, or at least place such an exorbitant value upon him, as amounted to a prohibition.

It will be seen then, that, notwithstanding the strong desire exhibited by members of the same family to be reunited, yet the difficulties which in most cases opposed the accomplishment of their wishes were of a nature to prevent their unconditional freedom. The rich man could generally redeem his relations; but after the grinding tyranny of the Ashantee supremacy, riches were far from abundant in the land.

Neither, at the time to which we refer, was the attainment of wealth within the reach of many. Confidence had not yet been completely established. The Ashantees, upon whom we were dependent for our principal supply of gold, were in the habit of visiting the coast for the purposes of trade in large parties, who, on account of the suspicion which still lurked in their minds, did not consider themselves altogether safe, unless under the protection of some of the principal chiefs or head men of the Fantee country. They therefore left their own country, consigned to some one of these, who acted as brokers, in carrying on their trade with the Europeans. This was a source of great emolument to the parties immediately employed, but had little effect in diffusing any general benefit. It, in fact, increased only the property of those who had the least need for it, and enabled them to increase still more the distance between them and the other classes of society, and to lay hold of those advantages which a superior position in its early stages never fails to place within their reach.

While this state of matters continued, the general body of the people who felt most the pressure of their separate bondage, had no opportunity of acquiring means to purchase their own redemption, or that of their relatives. They were therefore obliged to content themselves with the knowledge of their different situations, and to limit their intercourse to an occasional visit or message, as circumstances gave them opportunity. Upon these occasions they

would, in pure simplicity of heart, often seek
to bespeak a master's favour for a relation, by
trifling presents ; and by instigating the slave to
zeal for his master's service, and the master to
kindness, they endeavoured to keep alive such
mutual feelings of satisfaction and good-will, as
made the connection between them agreeable to
both. Where this good understanding did not
exist, and where the severity of the master rendered the slave's life miserable, recourse was often
had to some wealthy person, who had the reputation of being a good man, who was entreated
to purchase his redemption from the bad master,
and to make him his own slave ; and as the
services of a discontented slave were always unsatisfactory to the master, the latter generally
consented readily enough to his redemption.
Slaves and pawns had it thus very much in
their own power to make choice of their own
master, and this liberty of choice contributed
largely to bring together the different members
of a family under one master, and thus, by af-
fording free scope to the enjoyment of the
domestic affections, deprived slavery of its severest
sting.

This then was the first step which the full
protection given by the government enabled the

people to take—namely, the more general union of the different members of a family under the same roof, and the relief opened up to many from the severity of a bad master. As yet, however, there was no diminution in the extent of slavery. It was its quality alone which had been affected.

But the progress after this is now rapid. The great vigilance of the government in detecting, and its rigour in punishing acts of oppression, the frequent resort of aggrieved persons to the local authorities, and the ready and cheap redress of injuries, soon made the whole population perfectly familiar with the nature of the protection afforded them, and unwilling to submit to any wrong at the hands of their own chiefs. From the decision of these, appeals were frequent. The chiefs themselves, in consequence, had often occasion to resort to Cape Coast Castle, and had many opportunities, by their attendance in court, of comprehending more fully the broad principles of justice, and the necessity of enforcing them for the general good of society. They soon perceived that the governor's severity, which they had at first been inclined to regard as persecution, was dictated from an enlightened view of a necessary example, for the mainte-

nance of order, and the general tranquillity of
the country, in which they themselves had the
principal interest. A better and more cordial
understanding, which at length ripened into the
most perfect confidence and esteem, was the
result of a longer acquaintance.

The effect of all this was to bring the governor
prominently forward before the whole country in
his true position——as the federal head and protector of the allied chiefs, responsible for their
observance of treaties to the Ashantees, and
their defender against any unjust demands from
these——their mediator between each other, and
the general redresser of wrongs. The chiefs
began to regard themselves as so many officers
of government, to each of whom was entrusted
the administration of the affairs of his own
people, subject to the supervision of the governor, who, by the punishment of injustice, and
by heartily approving and rewarding a proper
discharge of their duties, soon managed to elicit
a strong desire to obtain his favour. If the
motives for this zeal were base, it was nevertheless attended with a more extensive distribution of justice, and the diffusion generally of
a more humane and equitable spirit. Instead
of a captious opposition, seeking insidiously to

overreach the law, and laying hold of every possible occasion to cause obstruction, and to limit the influences of good order, there was now, externally at least, a disposition which we believe in many cases to have been founded on a just appreciation of their real interests, to go hand-and-hand with the governor, and to give him every assistance in establishing and maintaining a more perfect system of justice than had hitherto guided their intercourse with each other.

Their ideas of justice, it is true, were not of that enlightened character which belongs to a higher standard of moral duty. They were still influenced by the prejudices of a dark superstition and traditionary customs, and required the watchful and resolute caution of a skilful reformer, whose care was as necessary in guarding against a too hasty innovation, as in rigidly enforcing the utmost degree of social progress which might safely be ventured upon.

Nor was the governor without a sufficient test of the state of public feeling upon these important points. The court (of which, at the time to which we refer, he was himself the judge) became a species of lecture-room, from which the principles of justice were disseminated far and wide throughout the country. It was daily crowded by listeners from the most distant districts under our jurisdiction, as well as by those close at hand. The practice of the chiefs being constantly surrounded by a large body of retainers, gave greater publicity to the doctrines inculcated, by the free access of all classes to a knowledge of the sentiments which influenced their government. The chief there learned that an injustice done in his judicial capacity would recoil upon himself; the master, that he owed duties to his slave, the neglect of which, or an undue severity, would lead to his unconditional emancipation; the slave, that though obedience was the badge of all his tribe, he was still the object of a care, which would shield him from oppression and vindicate his title to a kind and humane consideration; the husband, that his wife and the mother of his children was not a mere household drudge, the instrument of his gross passion, and his grosser cupidity, but that she was entitled to his love and his regard, and was intended to be the sharer of his joys and his sorrows; and the wife that she had been submitting to an unjust degradation, and that she could appeal successfully against the unworthy position allotted to her. Although it was not always possible to carry out the rules of moral duty to the extent that could be desired—and a mightier influence than that of the civil magistrate was necessary for their strict observance—yet the effect of the decisions in the court, and the general expositions with which they were attended, had a very sensible operation in ameliorating generally the social condition of the people.

The court also became a very successful, and not an invidious medium of attack upon their most objectionable laws and customs, as well as upon such of their superstitious observances as led to an unjust invasion of individual rights and liberties. The victims of their severe laws in reference to debt, of a false accusation, and of pretended crimes of which they had no evidence but their superstitious fears, or the oracular dictate of the Fetishman, of sorcery, witchcraft, and of a variety of superstitious offences, never applied in vain for protection. Any direct attack upon such dearly-cherished prejudices would have raised a perfect storm of opposition, and such watchwords as ever answer party purposes would soon have been heard, to intimate that persecution had begun. But when it was seen that the governor did not go out of his way to seek for cause of accusation, that he merely threw his protecting shield over one of themselves appealing against injuries inflicted for offences, of the commission of which they could produce no reasonable proof, they were obliged to acknowledge that he was actuated by a sense of justice, and not by direct hostility to their customs. By this indirect censure, and the tone of slighting ridicule with which their childish superstitions were treated, as if unworthy of a moment's serious consideration, many bad practices which at one time had been attended with very injurious consequences fell completely into contempt, and were laughed at and disavowed by those who still had faith in them, although they were ashamed to own it.

Sometimes during the investigation of circumstances connected with appeals to the court, cruel and barbarous practices were revealed, which were scarcely known to the Europeans to exist; but which were considered a necessary part of their religious observances, which could not be abolished without incurring the displeasure of the gods. The pertinacity with which ignorance hugs its absurd superstitions is well known, and appears to be in exact proportion to their absurdity. Abstract reasoning with such characters is perfectly out of place. An implicit faith in the benevolent intention of the law-giver, a consciousness of his general superiority, and of the advantages of obedience, occasional demonstrations of his power, and the certainty of punishment in withstanding it, are essential to the abolition of a confirmed custom. The prejudices in its favour will exist long after its fruits have been destroyed, and will only yield to time, and the influence of a new class of ideas arising out of a more comprehensive view of self-interest. As soon, then, as the governor had established sufficient confidence to afford a reasonable hope of success in putting down their most obnoxious practices, he cautiously led his attack against them. By frequent animadversions upon their iniquitous character, and the absolute necessity of abolishing them, by the announcement that he was only waiting for a favourable opportunity to do so effectually, he familiarized men's minds to their possible suppression at no distant period, and won over many to an acknowledgment of their unfitness; and when he perceived that he had thus sufficiently paved the way for an enactment upon the subject, he peremptorily commanded their discontinuance. This very possibly had not the desired effect, but it gave to their repetition the character of a punishable offence, made the greatest secrecy necessary to their commission, and subjected the perpetrators to punishment upon discovery.

The amount and nature of the public sympathy

consequent upon the punishment of the offender, afforded a perfect criterion of the seasonableness of the step; and thus the court served admirably the purposes of a pulse to indicate the extent of the reformation which the country was at any time capable of bearing, consistent with the degree of confidence in the government, without which no progressive improvement could be general. It was therefore politic not to endanger this confidence by rash and hasty legislation, which, however beneficial in reference to the point in question, was nevertheless to be avoided, if it prevented a greater good, by interrupting the course of gradual and steady advancement upon which the country had entered, as any interruption of this kind at the outset would have been fatal to our influence.

CHAPTER II.

General order and security — Its effect upon trade —
Employment given to the people—Progressive diffusion
of wealth—Extensive system of credit—Attributable to
the severity of the law of debt—The injurious tendency
counterbalanced by its advantages—Trade chiefly dependent on Ashantee — Oil trade — Condition of the
people.

HAVING in the foregoing chapter given, we
hope, an intelligible account of the nature of our
influence, of its extent, and its mode of development, the reader will have less difficulty in accounting for the rapid advancement now consequent
upon the establishment of those feelings of confidence and mutual good-will which we have represented as subsisting between the governor and the
governed. By this influence the most complete

protection and security were afforded to every one. The paths and thoroughfares of the country became as safe for the transmission of merchandize, and as free from interruptions of any description, as the best frequented roads of the most highly civilized countries of Europe. No police force, organized upon the principles of discipline which govern this important engine of civil government in a free country, can be compared in efficiency with that system of responsibility which made the chief accountable for the peace of his district, and for the orderly conduct of his dependants.

The patriarchal rule, which obtains in families, the assemblage of families under a chief, the vassalage of chiefs under a common superior, with the feelings of strict obedience, submission and clanship, strengthened and confirmed by superstitious observances, which exercise such a powerful control over those having faith in them, form altogether such a nicely graduated scale of accountability, that independence of action becomes impossible, and the detection of crime consequently easy. With this free scope for the full development of energy and enterprize, we are now to pursue the peculiar modes in which they principally exhibited themselves.

The Ashantees were not slow in perceiving that all danger of being obstructed and plundered was now at an end, and that the especial protection of a particular chief was no longer necessary. They were therefore glad to be relieved from the inconvenience of travelling in such large parties, and from the exorbitant profits which the chiefs received in name of brokerage for the simple transacting of their trade with the merchants. They soon discovered thousands eagerly seeking to be employed, and anxious to offer their services at a much more moderate rate; and they experienced much greater freedom of choice in this simple and unostentatious system of trade. On the other hand, the certainty of protection, and the profitable nature of mercantile speculation at the time, allured numbers to try their fortune as trading adventurers. Small capitalists invested what gold they had in goods, and either carried them into the interior, or sent them in charge of confidential agents to be sold.

The success of these petty adventurers had a magical effect in making this system general. Even the merchants themselves, finding that the quantity of goods thus sent for sale into the interior had a sensible influence in curtailing their own store trade, by preventing in a great measure the resort of the Ashantees to the coast, were obliged to yield to the current, and to carry on their business principally by means of agents employed in the same manner.

Instead of the dull, stagnant, lifeless appearance which the country presented some time before, the monotony of which was only varied occasionally by an act of gross outrage, or the sudden outbreak of an old hereditary feud, all was now cheerful bustle and activity. There was not a nook or corner of the land to which the enterprize of some sanguine trader had not led him. Every village had its festoons of Manchester cottons and China silks, hung up upon the walls of the houses, or round the trees in the market-place, to attract the attention and excite the cupidity of the villagers.

In the principal towns on the main line of communication with Ashantee, extensive depôts were formed, where every species of goods suited to the traffic might be got in abundance; and in Coomassie, the capital, many agents constantly resided, who received steady supplies of goods by an uninterrupted system of conveyance from the coast.

The land carriage of all this merchandize, in a country where beasts of burden are not used, gave employment to many thousands in transporting the goods. The porterage, considering the great distance of the journey, and the time occupied in accomplishing it, was exceedingly trifling; but the ignorance of the value of labour properly directed, and their natural distaste for a steady, regular and laborious employment, made them prefer occasional jobs of this description, which gratified also a rambling disposition, to agricultural pursuits, or any other occupation requiring fixed habits of application.

As yet, their absolute wants were few and their desires moderate. The simple supply of the necessaries of life was all that the bulk of the population cared about, and this the bounty of nature placed within the reach of a very small amount of labour. The prospect of elevating their condition by careful industry, had only yet been opened up to those engaged in trade, who perceived the road to wealth and consequence now plainly exposed to them. These eagerly pursued their advantages, perfectly alive to the important consequences of success, while the instruments of their traffic, the unreflecting carriers, were conscious of few wants to which the beasts of burden, whose province they had assumed, were not subject. On this account the diffusion of wealth although greatly extended beyond its former limit, was still partial, but rapidly progressive; for the numerous instances of independence suddenly acquired, could not but strike the dullest apprehension, and excite, in some measure, a more general spirit of emulation.

The condition of slavery, also, which attached to the greater part of those carriers was another reason for their want of ambition. They had in general been hired from a master, who received their wages, and only gave them out of their scanty allowance what was necessary for their subsistence. To such persons, the present movement held out little prospect of bettering their condition; and only those who, from their superior quickness of parts had given promise of achieving a more honourable position for themselves, and increased wealth for their masters, were afforded opportunities of seeking their own fortune.

It was the nature, however, of this system of trade by means of agents employed to sell goods in the interior upon the merchants' account, to become one of simple credit. The step between agency and the responsibility of a common debtor was so easy, and the latter liable to so much less misunderstanding, that credit soon became general. The natural result of this system of trust, was the extensive diffusion of property throughout every class of society, to a degree which can hardly be comprehended by one unacquainted with the peculiar partiality of the natives of the Gold Coast, and, we believe, of Africa generally, for pedling.   Men, women and children are indiscriminately infected with this passion, which absolutely assumes, from its inveteracy, the character of a confirmed malady.   One is at a loss to conceive where there is any room for buyers among such a nation of pedlers; and there is certainly no way of accounting for the disposal of such an endless exhibition of their petty wares, except upon the principle of barter. The foundation of the confidence upon which this general and extraordinary subdivision of credit is grounded, among a people by no means remarkable for their integrity, must, we believe, be sought for in the severity of the law of debt, which involves such an extensive responsibility, including that of the freedom of the debtor and his relations, rather than in the facile credulity of the people.

Owing to this peculiarity of their laws, the advantages of this system of general credit, as a means of improving their social condition, have been very doubtful; but we are inclined to think that its effect in creating artificial wants, and in forming new habits, and thereby exciting to their

gratification by industrious exertion, far outweighs
the temporary injustice and abuses which the
spirit of progress evoked by it must ultimately
redress. Its immediate effects, however, were
undoubtedly of a mixed character, dependent in
a great measure upon individual capacity and
integrity; for where credit was so general, education almost unknown, and the standard of moral
principle extremely low, it could not be, but that
much of this credit was misplaced, and that property was frequently squandered, as often by the
incapacity as by the unprincipled extravagance
of the debtor. But whatever the cause, the
result was the same—the implication of the innocent relations, who have been made available, to
raise the funds to liquidate the debt, either by
bondage as pawns, or by actual sale.

As a counterpoise, however, to the foolish and
reckless adventurers, who have thus entailed misery
upon themselves and families, there have been
others of a very different stamp; men who, by
cautious prudence and integrity, have acquired
the means of elevating the social position of themselves, and of redeeming from the bondage of a
former period their most distant relatives. As
these more than outnumbered the former, and as,
moreover, by the happy result of their exertions,

they exhibited in its proper light the legitimate fruits of honest dealing, the emulation which their success created, and the general aspirations which it raised for greater independence, greatly overbalanced the evils resulting from the abuse of their privilege. This preponderance became still more apparent as soon as it was known that by an appeal to the court, relations were relieved from all responsibility respecting debts incurred without their especial suretiship, as it put it beyond the power of every worthless character to impoverish and enslave his relations.

But the benefit of this protection was not so general as it might have been. The court only interfered upon application made to it. Public prejudice was still in favour of old customs. It was esteemed a disgrace to cast off a relation on account of debt, if the family had at all the means of paying it, and very seldom, except in the case of a confirmed and incorrigible prodigal, and where the liability was altogether beyond their means, did they withhold their support. The system of pawning therefore still continued. Even in cases where the creditor has failed to interest the debtor's family, and has in consequence been compelled to imprison him for the debt, they have finally yielded to the feelings of sympathy excited in his favour, and after allowing him time for correction and reflection, have helped him out of his troubles. But notwithstanding the influence of an established custom, in preventing the relief, which was put within their reach, being universally or even generally accepted, yet the knowledge that it might be had recourse to, had a very sensible effect in curtailing the extent of credit; and when it was seen that insolvent debtors obtained their discharge after a period of purgation, little more was needed to restrain credit within those limits which are essential to the interests of commerce, as well as to the steadiness and consistence of social progress.

By this useful limitation, and the removal of certain restrictions upon prices imposed by a self-constituted Board of Trade, the carrying system received its death-blow. The room for competition, which an unfettered traffic opened up, enabled those who preferred a sure store trade to make such a reduction of price, as induced the Ashantees to come to the coast, instead of making their purchases from the petty traffickers, or from the depôts in the interior. The greater choice of merchandize in the stores of the merchants, the presents which the traders were in the habit of receiving, and which eventually became an established perquisite, their little consideration of the value of time, and their consequent indifference about the length of their journey, combined with more consideration for themselves, and greater fairness of dealing than guided the transactions of adventurers, far removed from any sufficient control, all conspired to place the trade entirely upon a new footing. The consequence of the Ashantees becoming their own carriers, was to throw a very great number of persons out of employment, and to force them to seek another means of living.

Since the commencement of the carrying trade, they had become accustomed to many trifling luxuries within the reach of their scanty pay, to which they had formerly been strangers. These had now become absolutely necessary to them, and they were willing to turn their hands to any work, in order to obtain the means of procuring them. This certainly was a great step in advance; but the absence of any suitable occupation seemed on the point of consigning them once more to their original habits of perfect idleness, when the medium of circulation throughout the Fantee country was increased so rapidly, that an astonishing impetus was given to a branch of trade, which had not hitherto occupied a very prominent place in their attention. Gold-dust and ivory had been almost the sole articles of export. Neither of these commodities was found in great abundance within the countries under our jurisdiction, and our trade was, and is, principally dependent upon Ashantee. The only source of wealth was, therefore, confined to an interchange of the manufactures of Europe, for articles beyond the reach of labour to obtain them, and consequently beyond the reach of the mass of the population. Until labour found a marketable value, there was no prospect of the general amelioration of the condition of the people. Had gold been found in the soil of the country in sufficient quantities to render the search for it a steady and profitable occupation, it is possible that labour of this kind would have tended to improve the circumstances of the masses ; but the uncertainty of the result of labour of this description, and the reckless gambling spirit to which it invariably gives rise, are very unfavourable to moral improvement. On this account, we consider it particularly fortunate for the people of the Gold Coast, that the branch of industry to which their attention has been directed is one which, at the same time that it gives a good return for the labour expended, yet renders necessary habits of patient toil and application.

The manufacture of palm-oil, as giving employment to a great portion of the population, may be said to have been only known within the last fifteen years. It had been made in small quantities long before this period, but it had no general influence, nor do we think that it would have ever risen into the importance which it is now assuming, except for the extensive use of the circulating medium to which we have referred. Slaves, for some time, as being the staple of commerce, held the most conspicuous place as a test of computation, and an article was ordinarily reckoned at the value of one, two, or more slaves. But the immense variety of circumstances which depreciated their value or otherwise, made it of such a relative quality, that even the classification into prime, good, bad, and indifferent, conveyed but a doubtful and indefinite idea of their true worth.

The assumption of gold-dust as the standard of value, was, therefore, highly conducive to the interests of trade; but its supply was so limited, and so little diffused, as to render it altogether inadequate as a medium of circulation. The deficiency was attempted to be made up, by means of various articles of trade, which were passed from hand to hand at the market price at the time, or for such value as might be agreed upon between the payer and receiver. These articles, however, were generally of a very perishable nature, and unless required for immediate consumption, of little use to the person receiving them. As long as this state of things continued, and there was no ready and convertible price for labour of easy access, there was little inducement to work; but when labour could be very profitably employed in the manufacture of an article of great consumption, for which there was always a ready market, and which was paid in a commodity capable of great subdivision, and in constant use as the circulating medium of an extensive district of the country, motives for exertion were only limited by the extent of desire.

The introduction of the cowrie-shell and its application to this purpose supplied the desideratum necessary for the prosecution of the trade in palm-oil, the supply of which is found to fluctuate according to the supply of the cowries. If these have been exhausted in the stores of the merchants, no oil is brought to the market unless in such small quantities as may be required for immediate consumption; and although the manufacture of oil may go on in the meantime, in the expectation of new importations of cowries, yet if these be long delayed, the activity of the labourer slackens and finally ceases; the object of his labour being to obtain what to him is tantamount to ready cash, which he can apply in any manner he thinks fit.

The reader will have some idea of the utility of this article as a circulating medium, when we state that the annual importation of cowries is steadily increasing, and that it at present amounts to one hundred and fifty tons per annum. When he is farther informed that a ton of good cowries is equivalent to three hundred and sixty dollars, that two thousand four hundred shells go to the dollar, and that there are consequently eight hundred and sixty-four thousand cowries in a ton, he will more readily comprehend the facilities of exchange, and the great encouragement which it gives to industry. It would be impossible at present even to conjecture with any degree of probability the extent to which this importation of a very serviceable currency might be carried, without affecting its circulating value ; but the sudden and extraordinary increase of late years, has had no effect in deteriorating them, and the increased demand keeps pace with the supply—in other words, a sufficient marketable equivalent for labour has not yet been supplied, as the resources of the country and the energies of the people are only in their first stages of development. How these will ultimately be operated upon, with the best result, it is at present too soon to determine, and must depend upon the market which they find for their labour, and the judgment with which it is directed.

As yet, cowries are only in use throughout a comparatively small portion of the Gold Coast; and where they are not already introduced, a strong prejudice exists against them. In Ashantee it is forbidden to sell or pass them at all, under very severe penalties; the impression being, that their introduction and use might have an injurious effect in diminishing the extent of the collections of gold-dust. Along the whole line of coast also to the westward of Anamaboe, cowries are little used, and do not pass current in the markets; gold-dust, silver, and copper coins being the only medium of circulation. Owing to the expenditure of the government at Cape Coast, the circulation of money and gold of the country almost suffice for the present exigencies of the people, and hold out the necessary inducement for labour; but where there is nothing extraneous to the gold-dust, the energy of the people is cramped for want of a sufficiently diffusive currency.

We accordingly find that the condition of the natives in those parts is much more stationary, and that, notwithstanding their greater attention to the collection of gold, and the superior abundance of this valuable mineral in these districts, they are nevertheless excluded from many comforts which are now within the reach of all who devote their labour to the cultivation of the produce of the country, and who readily find a marketable price for it. Every branch of trade and industry known to the people has been influenced in an extraordinary manner, by adopting this currency; but greater incentives are still wanting to call forth the energies of the people generally, for many still remain sunk in a sluggish indifference, from which, we fear, they can only be roused by education.

CHAPTER III.

Disinclination for improvement—Difficulty of overcoming
prejudices—Toleration of the government— Anomalies
observable in society, and in individual character—
Compulsory observance of order—Gives rise to commercial enterprise — Growing taste for the habits of
civilized life—Moral virtues neglected— Establishment
of a school—Arrival of a Christian missionary upon the
coast.

IF a benevolent government, with moral influence sufficient to obtain general obedience, and to
give protection and security to all, a fair measure
of commercial prosperity, a full abundance of the
necessaries of life, with the means of supplying
many artificial wants placed within the reach of
every class, were the only requisites for the social
elevation of a people, the natives of the Gold

Coast had now a favourable opportunity of entering upon this career. But something more is necessary to raise a people from a state of great moral degradation. Without the consciousness of their own debasement, and a desire for their own advancement, the most favourable circumstances will be unavailing; and the experience of all history shows that this feeling and this desire do not arise naturally.

The human mind is not a soil, where ideas common to an in a civilized state spring up spontaneously. Not a field in the material world requires more diligent culture. The weeds which rankle there are only a type of the tendency, not of the extent of human depravity. The former germinate, flourish, wither, die and are renewed. The latter knows no winter, no season of frigid inaction, in which the principle of vitality and development is suspended. Its growth is continuous, strengthening with man's strength, and transmitted through successive generations with a continually increasing bent, and a more confirmed and instinctive impulse. And as the natural field has not any inherent power to substitute the wheat for the tares, so neither has the mind of man the capacity of originating and carrying out into practice ideas of an opposite tendency from its natural and confirmed bent, without the addition of some external influence.

The ordinary operation of this influence is certainly through the medium of the senses, and reflection upon the effects produced upon them; for what by some of the heathen philosophers, with an indistinct glimmering of the truth, has been denominated "the divine breathing," by modern infidels the result of reason affecting the moral principle, and by revelation the inspiration of the Holy Ghost, has little permanent effect upon the actions of men in their natural state; and for these simple reasons, that in the one case a certain degree of moral advancement is necessary to qualify men to deduce salutary rules of life from tracing effects to their original cause; and in the other, where the Scriptures have not been received as a revelation from heaven, the importation of a divine influence has been misunderstood, has consequently not been cherished, and has therefore resembled in its motions, rather the eccentricity of the comet than the steady undeviating course of the sun.

It is then to the slow process of mental culture, the result of compulsion in its first stages, that we are to look for a substitution of one class of ideas for another, and for the change of habits and principles upon which this substitution is founded. But it is well known, that nothing but the strong hand of power and a clearer view of self-interest can put down a cherished custom and remove a confirmed habit. Even against power and self-interest, the prejudices of the old, who have grown grey in the practice of customs established by prescription, the opposition of monopolist traders in the abuses of society, the superstitious fears of some, the ridicule of others, and the natural disinclination for change in all, invariably maintain an obstinate struggle.

Upon the Gold Coast, the government has very wisely made no attack upon customs which did not interfere with the rights and liberties of individuals, and has only so far meddled with their laws, as to infuse into them a more humane spirit; ameliorating some without abolishing them, and consigning others to a gradual oblivion, by exposing their unfitness for the advancing condition of social progress. This spirit of toleration has consequently left the battle of civilization to be fought, principally by the influence of opinion; and this opinion being moulded, not by any general system of education calculated to conduce, with slight modifications, according to the structure of individual minds, to one great homogeneous result; but being the effect of a variety of influences acting partially upon society, its operation has, of course, been as partial as their application.

We accordingly find the most incongruous anomalies in the general aspect of society; and not
only in general society, but, according to our
views of consistent keeping in character, the
strangest inconsistencies in the same individual.
This is to be accounted for by his accidental
training for his particular occupation, and the
opportunities which he has had of associating with
and observing the conduct of men more civilized
than himself. Having called into action particular
qualities of the mind, and drawn his attention to a
special round of duties, particular faculties have
been improved and certain observances respected,
while other mental qualities have remained
perfectly fallow, and other duties, equally important, have been disregarded, as they were not called
into operation, and did not fall within the range of
his observation.

We have thus a root of barbarism with a branch
of civilization; the crab and the apple growing
side by side, upon the same tree, and in proportions varying with the opportunities and inclination
to receive new grafts. If the latter were as general
as the former, advancement would be much more
rapid; but nothing but a personal experience of
self-interest appears to have any influence in
moulding the will to seek voluntarily a change of
condition. The pleasure of doing nothing has

such a narcotic influence upon the human faculties, that the more it is indulged in, the more inveterately is it cherished, until the whole man is steeped in such a lethargic stupor that it is next to impossible to rouse him. Where the bounty of Providence supplies the actual wants of life almost without the necessity of labour, and where, moreover, the climate has an enervating influence upon the human frame, this luxurious dream of listless inactivity appears to become the chief pleasure of existence. For this reason, the allurements to exertion require to be kept continually pressing upon them, and the senses to be constantly stimulated by new and powerful incentives. From this cause it is, that we find so much indifference, and even dislike to engage in occasional occupations, which would appear to us, from the remuneration given, to hold out considerable inducements; but he fact is, this occupation not being continuous, and heir condition not being permanently affected by it, their ordinary wants. moreover, not rendering it necessary for their supply, the temporary benefit is not considered worth the exertion required to obtain it.

To rouse the energies of any people long buried in sloth, there must be an adequate inducement in the immediate and permanent amelioration of their condition, and this inducement must come home in a tangible form to the general body. The least attention to the course of social progress in this country, and not in this country alone, but in every other country, attests this truth. But for the fear of punishment, which would entail upon the perpetrator of an injustice a greater injury than the possible advantage which he might obtain from its commission, the natives of the Gold Coast would have continued to hunt, persecute, and worry each other until this very hour. No abstract love of justice, no feelings of compassion, were capable of exercising any restraint. The personal consequences of criminality alone had the power to enforce anything like an observance of justice, and the incessant disregard even of this restraint, at the commencement, is a sufficient proof that the golden rule of doing to others as we would that they should do unto us, is not one of natural growth.

The first step, then, was pure compulsion; but it was the introduction of the fine point of the wedge, which communicated an aptitude for its deeper insertion, and which did not leave the whole work to be done by the force of external application. The advantages of a purer administration of justice soon became apparent to society. It was seen that its practice was not merely a negative good, relieving men from the consequences of disobedience; but that a positive benefit to the public flowed from it. This benefit once experienced became indispensable, and notwithstanding the interested opposition of individuals, infused such a general spirit, not of acquiescence only, but of eagerness to secure and render it permanent, that what had at first been introduced by force, was cherished from choice and maintained from motives of self-interest. Here was the first pliable adaptation of the cleft to the wedge, which prepared the way for a more extensive opening upon the next application of pressure from without; and as this first step, the observance of justice and consequent order and tranquillity, was binding on all, its influence was general, and its effects naturally exhibited in the diffusion of a more humane spirit throughout every class of society.

This, however, is the only improvement of universal application. Whatever other changes have been wrought have been partial, and in exact proportion in their nature and extent to the means employed for their development. The next most general benefit was the result of the protection and security now enjoyed by all, which gave ample scope for commercial enterprise. It consisted in a more extensive diffusion of wealth, increased liberty in proportion to this wealth, and an ambition, among those who had been most successful, to assume the habits and acquire the tastes of civilized life.

The measure of success attending those enterprises became also the measure of individual advancement, which, from the nature of the cause, produced, as a matter of course, an endless variety of effect. We consequently find all degrees of progress, from the dull and sluggish bushman, who has just been shamed into the necessary exertion to acquire means to purchase a cloth to cover himself, to the intelligent and enterprising merchant, who is receiving his consignments of thousands from Europe.

It will be observed, however, that the incentives hitherto noticed, addressed themselves principally to a particular class of the affections, calling into exercise only those faculties requisite for the successful management of their traffic. This, of course, left a very extensive field perfectly untilled. While it excited ambition, exercised the judgment, and generally sharpened the intellectual faculties, it had little influence upon the moral powers of the mind, except to the extent which a more enlarged view of personal interest has upon human conduct, which is consequently rather an effect of the intellect than of the moral principle. Actions based upon this foundation, will be in correspondence with the degree of enlightenment of the individual, thereby rendering a very high degree of mental cultivation essential to the practice of pure morality. It is a well-established fact, however, that men have never been able fully to act up to their own convictions of right, when they have assumed reason only for their guide. A strong temptation, where the risk of detection or of injury appears impossible and doubtful, has often proved too much for the highest effort of mere reason to resist. Such being the case with men of the most highly cultivated intellect, what have we a right to expect from a people just emerging from the thraldom of body and of mind which we have represented? With an education limited to traditionary laws and customs, generally of a corrupt and immoral nature, with a superstitious religion, which makes no pretension to be a moral guide of conduct; without even the lessons of experience, and with no higher standard of obedience than the will of the civil magistrate, whose means of information, and whose powers of punishment are by no means commensurate with the wants of society, is it to be wondered at that the moral virtues have not a very prominent place in their regard?

To such a people, offences punishable by law only appear criminal; and even then, the detection of the offence, rather than the offence itself, constitutes the crime. Offences and vices not generally cognizable by the civil magistrate, therefore, carry with them little degradation, and are scarcely regarded in a derogatory point of view. Lying, prevarication, low cunning, breach of engagements, and trick and artifice of every deecription, are with them legitimate weapons in the battle of life. Intemperance, excess, lewdness, strifes, abusiveness, and malice predominate in the general character; and all these vicious practices only give way in proportion to the experience of their injurious effects upon their interest.

This ought to excite no astonishment in the mind of the candid and rational observer, neither can it for a moment be accepted as an argument in favour of any constitutional inferiority of race, as it is as natural a result of the tendency of the human mind, under the influences of the circumstances which have affected their condition, as that "the earth bringeth forth fruit of herself; first the blade, then the ear, after that the full corn in the ear."

The degeneracy of a people is no doubt more or less affected by the circumstances of their condition. It attaches equally to their moral and physical nature; and we will not deny but that the African may, through ages of progressive deterioration, have acquired a deeper moral taint than other races more favourably circumstanced. The indiscretion of a parent entails a constitutional taint upon his offspring to the third and fourth generations. We are not sufficiently acquainted with physiology to know whether the converse of this holds true, but we should think so—namely, that a careful attention to regimen, and an abstinence from predisposing causes, will, in the course of the same number of generations, eradicate this taint. If this be the case in the physical, it will also hold good in the moral world; the difficulty of removal always being in proportion to the duration of the disease before its attempted remedy. From this it would follow, that by suitable training, good laws and an enlightened Christian education, the most degraded of the African tribes may, in the course of some generations, attain an equality of standard with any other race of men whatever.

When we mention the low moral standard, then, of the mass of the Gold Coast population, we by no means do so as a reproach to them, nor can we consider it as such: the reproach is with those who have traded in their vices and made a profit of them.

The philanthropic exertions of England in behalf of Africa have, it is true, of late years, been attested by sacrifices which leave no doubt of their sincerity; but we cannot avoid remarking that these exertions have been much more conspicuous for their zeal, than for their wisdom.

Had a tithe of the money which, as far as any permanent advantage to Africa is concerned, has been fruitlessly expended in the Niger Expedition, been devoted to increase the means of our judicial power, and to the establishment of schools throughout the very extensive districts claiming our protection upon the Gold Coast, we do not hesitate to affirm, that, even by this time, the predominant character of the people would have assumed the stamp of an incipient civilization; but here, where the result was certain, and where the greatest facility was afforded for the introduction of every species of improvement, the efforts of the government to instruct the people have been confined to the establishment of a school at Cape Coast, and the occasional presence of a chaplain in the castle. Even these most inadequate means of instruction have been irregular and uncertain.

A school was not established until 1816, and since then it has been subject to various interruptions; at one time broken up on account of war, at another neglected through the indifference of governors and the total disregard of the European residents, and only kept from entire disruption by an occasional fit of zeal on the part of a new superintendent. The state of the country, also, until 1830, was much too unsettled to allow time for any thought but that of self-preservation. The interest taken by Sir Charles M'Carthy in the improvement of the country induced him to give his particular patronage to the school, and attracted to it for a short time a momentary success;* but the events which followed put all such thoughts from men's minds.

After the treaty of peace with Ashantee had been concluded, the government, which had devolved upon the merchants again, took no interest in the education of the people ; but the means at their disposal were altogether so limited, that the system of instruction pursued was only calculated to impart a very moderate degree of knowledge. Reading, writing, and arithmetic, with a very imperfect acquaintance with the principles of the Christian religion, constituted the full extent of the school education. It enabled young men to keep memoranda, copy papers and accounts, to superintend the discharging of cargo from vessels, oversee out-of-door work, and such simple employments ; but it did not qualify them for conducting a merchant's

---

* Sir Charles persuaded the principal chiefs to send one of their sons to the school at Cape Coast. This measure has, in one or two instances, produced excellent results, especially at Dominassie, where the education thus given to the son of the chief, Amissah, became instrumental in preparing the people of that village for the introduction of the Gospel.

business; although, by attention on the part of an employer, who gave himself the trouble to devote a little pains to the subject, and by diligence and docility on the part of the young men, several acquired a sufficient knowledge of book-keeping to become, at first, factors and clerks to the merchants; and, finally, to carry on business on their own account. The prejudices entertained against education, at first limited the scholars to the children of persons in the employment of the government; some of whom had the penetration to foresee its prospective advantages, while others considered that by sending their children to school, they were conferring an obligation upon, and would therefore enjoy, in a higher degree, the favour of their employers. An education of this description, however, was not calculated to have any very important influence upon the life of the individual. By elevating his position, enlarging his ideas, exciting his ambition, and placing upon the result of his actions a more important stake, affecting permanently his interest, he certainly acquired a superior degree of rectitude of conduct; but as, generally speaking, he was guided by what appeared most advantageous for his temporal advancement, it partook of all the imperfections of his individual judgment, and was the semblance rather than the reality of probity. It was not until 1835 that any attempt was made to introduce Christianity among the natives of the Gold Coast. The sound of the Gospel had seldom echoed beyond the walls of the castle, and even within this circumscribed limit it was confined to a formal repetition of church services, and an occasional discourse, delivered in a tongue not generally intelligible, and without an interpreter. To have expected much fruit from such a system of culture would have been contrary to all experience. In the minds of a few, the truths of Christianity left a salutary impression, and created a desire for greater enlightenment; but with the generality, even of such as had the opportunity, they had entered the ears without awakening the sense or touching the heart, and were incapable of uprooting the feelings of superstition which were naturally engendered by constant intercourse with friends and relations given to the practice of idolatry. The moral darkness of the people was consequently almost universal, when the attention of the Wesleyan Society was attracted to this part of the world. Their first missionary arrived here in 1835, and since then the exertions of this Christian society have been unremitting, and attended with results which, with a glance at the general effect of the other ameliorating influences which have been mentioned, will very appropriately close this branch of our subject.

CHAPTER IV.

The difficulties the first missionary had to struggle against,
from ignorance of the language — Misapprehensions
respecting Christianity — Persecution averted by the
government — Desertion of the missionary service —
Similar effects of the first propagation of Christianity
in other parts of the world—The Wesleyan Society—
Sacrifices made by many of the uneducated adult Christians—Their firmness and austerity.

THE great difficulty which presents itself to the
first European missionary, upon his arrival in such
a country as the Gold Coast, is his inability to
convey an intelligible impression of his meaning
to the minds of his hearers. He is obliged to
have recourse to the unsatisfactory medium of an
interpreter, himself but very imperfectly acquainted
with the nature of the doctrines which he is
called upon to expound. At the time to which we

refer, the knowledge of the English language was confined to a broken conversational dialect, also in very limited use, and only adapted to the most ordinary interchange of ideas, and the common traffic of life. Even within this small compass, it was often inadequate, without the assistance of intelligible acts, and significant pantomime, which could have no place in the interpretation of the doctrines of the Christian religion. The school at Cape Coast Castle, it is true, had sent forth, at different times, a few young men acquainted with the ordinary branches of a school education, and versed in some degree in the familiar, although by no means grammatical, use of the English language; but it is a remarkable fact, that, with some rare exceptions, the generality of these, for want of any adequate employment, or from habits of a low and debasing nature, sank to the level of the uninstructed natives, and lost, in a great measure, even the traces of their early education. The exceptions to this unworthy fate, were such as had been taken from the school into some of the government offices, or into the employment of such of the merchants as required the services of a clerk or factor.

In those times, however, the whole trade of the coast was very insignificant, and confined to so few, that there was but little room for employment from this source. Limited therefore as was the supply, both in quality and quantity, of educated native talent, it was nevertheless greater than the demand; for to serve the purposes of petty trafficking, to which a system of credit had given rise, the knowledge of reading and writing and figures, unassociated with any higher degree of moral rectitude, was very justly considered, in many instances, a disqualification. The rarity of this knowledge had a tendency to excite, in the minds of those who had obtained it, an exaggerated idea of their superiority over others. With all the self-sufficiency of ignorance, they conceived that they had surmounted the barrier which divided the uninstructed African from the enlightened European; that their education, which was little more than mechanical, and their assumption, in part, of the habits and the dress of the white man, elevated them at once into something of an equality of position; that these adventitious circumstances alone constituted the chief essentials in the formation of a civilized being, and that nothing else was necessary to acquire the distinctive characteristic of what they emphatically term " a white man," than the possession of certain external advantages, which they had been in the habit of seeing the Europeans enjoying. They had a most imperfect idea of the infinite variety of gradations in the scale of civilization, and of the qualifications necessary for particular stages of advancement, and considered themselves fit for any situation which fortune might throw in their way.

If such was the self-complacent satisfaction with which these persons were inclined to regard themselves, the effect upon the vulgar was even more impressive. In the eyes of many, there was a virtue in the very coat and breeches—which typified the wearer, and invested him—although void of any moral or intellectual superiority over others—with a mysterious profundity of knowledge and information, which could not be contemplated without inspiring a certain degree of awe in the mind of the beholder. Their acquaintance with the occupations of Europeans was confined to the service of the government and commerce. As these called for the exercise of but little bodily exertion, they believed it to be a peculiar privilege of education to exempt them from labour. It seemed derogatory to their newly-acquired character to engage in any industrious manual occupation, which was only considered fit for slaves. Commerce alone was therefore regarded as an eligible road to a position in society. The effect of this misconception of their own position and present capabilities, as well as of the very erroneous views respecting their acquirements entertained by others, was most injurious to the cause of civilization. These errors were a prolific source of unprincipled extravagance, dishonourable artifice, idle indulgence, and grievous disappointment on the part of the one ; and of misplaced confidence, fruitless labours, duped credulity, and a consequent distaste for anything with the garb of civilization being introduced among the people, on the part of the other.

On this account it was, that a school education was accounted a disqualification. It fostered ideas of expense above their means, induced them to seek the gratification of their tastes, regardless of the consequences, enabled them to minister to their wants by the credulous simplicity of the ignorant, and ended by involving their relations in debt and bondage. It was no wonder, then, that the general body of the Africans, who had been watching the result of what they had reason to consider an European education, should, with such pregnant examples before their eyes, come to the conclusion, that " the school was a very good thing for white men, but not for black." Even in this very form of expression, we have an admission of the advantages of education, at the same time that its fruits, as exhibited among their own countrymen, seemed to bear them out in this opinion, that it was not adapted for them ; and if we add to the effect of this unfortunate result in influencing the public mind, the natural disinclination of a people to change the practice of their fathers, we shall be able to form some estimate of the opposition which the first missionaries had to encounter.

Their difficulties would have even been much greater than they were, except for the assistance which they received in expounding the Scriptures through the medium of some of those natives who had received their education in the castle.

These interpreters being already formed to their hand, gave an advantage of at least ten years labour; and thus the school, inefficiently and irregularly as it had been conducted, nevertheless produced a few young men, who became most useful pioneers in the missionary cause, and supplied the place of school teachers, until such time as they were able to employ youth of their own rearing. The pay given by the missionaries to the young men whom they employed as teachers, being fully equal to that given by the merchants, and a greater number of them being required for this service, the missionary employment became an object of ambition with many, as much, we are afraid, in many instances, for the sake of the loaves and fishes, as from a sincere and earnest desire to promote the cause of Christianity. This inducement drew a number of the best educated natives within the pale of the society; while the building of chapels, and other necessary works contingent upon the introduction of new and large establishments into the country, gave employment to a numerous staff of masons, carpenters and labourers, who, in like manner, swelled the ranks of the Christian community.

It would be uncharitable to suppose this conversion only apparent, or to assign it, even in a great measure, to mercenary and selfish motives; but the historian of such a movement must not lose sight of the tendencies of human nature; and when he finds these conducing to a result in many external respects analogous to the effect of religion, upon the life and conduct of men, he must impartially lay bare all the causes which appear to have operated in bringing about this end, as well as the effects produced by the removal of these causes and the substitution of new motives for exertion. While the bait of employment then attracted numbers to the Wesleyan Chapels, the promulgation of doctrines so new and unexpected aroused their attention, and led to speculation of a very mixed and ill-defined character, partaking naturally of the peculiarities inseparable from their social position, and the superstitious ideas and

observances to which the generality of them had
been accustomed. Little habituated to contemplate
the operations of the mind, and to deduce rules of
action from attention to them ; regardless also of
the heart as a spring, from which flow the issues
of life, they were more intent on discovering something in the new doctrine which would improve
their temporal condition, than on probing the
weaknesses of their nature, with the view of
reformation and amendment.

The material world had, as yet at least, a far
stronger hold upon their affections than the
spiritual, and all their notions of advantage to be
derived from the introduction of Christianity were
coloured by this prevailing tint. Texts of Scripture
that seemed to bear some reference to the peculiar
situation of individuals were wrested to suit their
views, and to minister to their inclinations and
wants.   To the slave, oppressed perhaps by the
severity of a rigid task-master, the announcement
that all men were equal before God, carried with
it a belief that his temporal bonds were dissolved,
and that he should no longer be subjected to
labour ; to woman, hitherto the drudge of man,
living in the outskirts of his affection, and sharing
with many rivals a cold and divided attention, the
command " to love, to comfort, to honour, and to
keep her in sickness and in health, and forsaking

all others, to keep only to her," must have opened up a vision of bliss for which the wildest freaks of her imagination had never prepared her; to the African, generally the object of supercilious scorn, of mocking irony, or of haughty indifference to the self-sufficient European, it must have been some satisfaction to learn that Christianity presented a neutral ground, upon which both races, laying aside the prejudices of birth, might harmoniously unite in one common brotherhood. These were advantages palpable to all, if they could only be realized, and the easy credulity of the ignorant unhesitatingly believed this to be extremely possible.

Much misconception was the consequence of thus referring the promises of Scripture to temporal affairs. Instead of drawing from them lessons of duty and correctives against the evil passions and appetites of human nature, they looked upon them as intended to subvert at once the whole established order of society, and to compel men, by the irresistible force of a stern necessity, to release them from all inconveniences attached to their position, without waiting for the influences of a great moral agency to convince the understanding, enlighten the judgment, purify the heart, and bring forth the fruits consequent upon this change.

These erroneous impressions aroused a spirit of

opposition, and sometimes of persecution, on the part of those whose interests appeared likely to suffer from such a sweeping revolution ; and but for the controling power of the local government, the missionaries would have been forcibly ejected from the country.   By its influence, toleration was established ; and whatever may have been the extent to which resistance was carried privately in families, no case of forcible restraint ever came within the knowledge of the government, without its authors being punished.   To this first outburst succeeded a period of quiet indifference.   With the cessation of persecution, zeal for conversion ceased also.   Time and a juster view of the scope of Christianity had removed many of those wild and visionary chimeras, which at first view had appeared easily attainable by all who embraced it ; and when it was found that it did not release them from the obligations which they owed to society, the work of proselytism went on much more slowly.   The converts were nearly limited to such as were connected directly or indirectly with the missionary service.   Exhorters and teachers, bricklayers, carpenters, and labourers, domestics of every grade, with the wives and sometimes the relations of these, and others in the pay of the society, constituted the great bulk of their congregation.

The Wesleyan system of church discipline being

strict, and expulsion from the ranks of the society consequent upon any known and glaring breach of the moral duties; the supervision, moreover, which they habitually exercise over the individual members being narrow, jealous, and inquisitive, a strong obligation rests upon them to conform to the rules of a Christian life. This obligation became more imperative, when expulsion from the society carried with it deprivation of office, and forfeiture of the pecuniary benefits which they were enjoying. Owing to this watchfulness, and the consequences to their temporal interests of any deviation from the prescribed duties required of them, the Christian community bore outwardly, at least, all the marks of sincerity of profession.

Where the result is satisfactory, it is not for man, perhaps, to pry too curiously into the secret motives of the heart, and to lay bare springs of action unknown to, at least unacknowledged by, the agents themselves; but where circumstances indicate the presence of other and contrary principles, we are constrained to believe that many of the converts were either labouring under a hypocritical delusion, or that the frailty of human nature exhibited itself with an uniformity of weakness truly humiliating and deplorable. This severity of expression, little consistent with the feelings of good-will and charity with which we are inclined to view every indication of progress in the country, is rendered necessary by the fact, that a neglect of Christian duties has almost invariably attended worldly advancement, and a return to lewd and immoral practices has as constantly followed dismissal from, or relinquishment of, the missionary employment.

The profits of trade, which of late years has received an extraordinary development, as much from the progress of education, as from the increased security derived from a more extensive dissemination of justice, held out such inducements to the best instructed natives, that the service of the missionary society, as a source of emolument, became altogether secondary. The facility with which credit could be obtained, placed this advantage within the reach of every person of moderate acquirements and of respectable character, and the consequence was that one by one, the most valuable servants of the society were enticed into mercantile employments, in the prosecution of which they lost that moral rectitude and pious deportment which had appeared to characterise their previous conduct.

So general was this course, that it almost assumed the form of a regular system. First, a season of quiet painstaking in the service of the missionaries, marked by a scrupulous, sometimes even an ostentatious observance of their religious duties; then an ambitious longing to become traders, with the command of property in their hands; afterwards dissatisfaction with the amount of their salaries, and a grumble for more pay; and finally, the abandonment of the service, and most generally at the same time an abandonment of the virtuous principles which hitherto had been supposed, at least, to have been the guide of their lives. Such a result we acknowledge to be perfectly compatible with sincerity. It is only too common an occurrence for man, when he omits to cherish incessantly the virtues which adorn the Christian character; and no one who has paid any attention to the deceitfulness of his own heart, will hazard the uncharitable opinion, that the former life of such men was either hypocritical or immoral. At the same time, we cannot shut our eyes to the fact, that there are only a very few exceptions to a general relapse into immorality, when motives of personal interest no longer bound the members to attention to their system of discipline.

There are exceptions, however, and highly honourable ones; some among the best-educated classes of the society, and more—to their great honour be it said—among humble artizans and workmen, who know neither how to read nor write. It is lamentable, however, to have to state, that many of the best-educated and most intelligent men, who, some years ago, were most distinguished for zeal for Christianity, and who occupied the first rank among the office-bearers of the society, are now living without its pale, while the offices are filled by an inferior class.

But the loss of membership by no means implies a return to idolatrous practices. With some of the most ignorant, whose comprehension of the object of Christianity had never been very definite, and whose worship, although addressed to the true God, was still tinctured more by the spirit of superstition than of a rational faith, this relapse was not uncommon ; but the more enlightened backsliders could not even lay hold of this miserable refuge from the upbraidings of conscience. Their convictions had been too strong, and their experience of the peaceable fruits of a life consistent with those convictions so agreeable, that its remembrance haunted their minds, poisoning their joys, and driving them to seek for its oblivion in excitements of a sinful and debasing character. Others of them, without sinking to this degradation, retaining a remorseful consciousness of their fall, and halting with all the misery of indecision between a return to duty, and the pleasures of sinful indulgence, continued to frequent the chapels, and to turn such looks of lingering regret upon the position which they had forfeited, as we may suppose our first parents to have turned to the Garden of Eden after their expulsion.

Humiliating as this exposition of the progress of Christianity undoubtedly is, it will occasion no surprise to the observant student of human nature. He will remember by what slow degrees a just conception of the pure precepts of the Gospel, as a guide of life, dawned upon the earliest converts ; how, even among the Apostles themselves, it was found necessary to prevent misconstruction, and to warn them against grafting them upon, and making them subservient to, the ideas and practices of the state of society, and the religious observances to which they had been accustomed ; how much difficulty the early churches of Asia found in making a complete separation between their ancient idolatry and their new faith ; what necessity there was for an unremitting supervision by faithful and zealous teachers ; and with what a fatal facility they relapsed into lukewarmness and idolatry, when this supervision slackened or was removed. He will bear in mind the number of centuries through which the churches of Europe presented nothing better than a gross superstition, occupied with forms and observances, without regarding the influences of true religion upon the conduct. He will not forget the effect of early habits and impressions, and with how much difficulty the human mind emancipates itself from these, more especially in a state of society where the individual is living daily exposed to a continuance of those influences ; and when he adds to these considerations the allurements of vice, the low standard of morality generally prevalent in the country, association with friends and relations still living in the practice of idolatry, the irregularity observable in the conduct of many of the Europeans, whom they have been taught to respect, and the general indifference with which a breach of the moral duties is regarded, he will not be astonished that a Christian church in its purity does not at once start into existence in the midst of so many conflicting elements.

But while the Christian philanthropist will find much need for the exercise of a patient faith in the final triumph of the truths of the Gospel, and will see occasion to check a too sanguine expectation of their speedy fulfilment, we are not at all inclined to undervalue the good which has been effected. Such a work as the conversion of a people from the grossest superstition to the pure morality of a Christian life, has hitherto been, and will continue to be—as far, at least, as we may judge from past experience—the result of a long series of years of gradual progress necessary for the development of the reflective powers of the mind. Individual and sudden conversions no doubt take place, and in many instances they may be followed by a consistent life; but it appears to us that these will occur much more rarely among rude and illiterate men than among an educated people, with whom the seeds of religion, long dormant in the heart, and scarcely known to exist at all, will often be quickened into vitality by sudden and unexpected interpositions of Providence.

It would be presumptuous to think of assigning limits for the operations of the Spirit, or of prescribing the manner in which they may be manifested. The truth, which may have escaped the penetration of the philosopher, has oftentimes dawned upon the mind of the clown. Judging, however, from the history of the past, we conceive that we are borne out in the opinion that, where the knowledge of letters is limited to a few, and where, consequently, the diffusion of knowledge is far from general, the ideas of the masses respecting Christianity will be vague and erroneous, their religious observances will be tinged with superstition, and more attention will be paid to the form than to the power of godliness. We must not therefore be astonished, if what we see presented as the result of the operations of the Wesleyan missionaries upon the coast, should confirm this opinion. They number, doubtless, among their converts some sincere, rational and consistent Christians; while others, imagining that some great good must flow from their worshiping the God of a people so favoured as the white men, join in the offices of religion with the same vague and indefinite ideas as prompted Peter on the Mount of Transfiguration to exclaim, " It is good for us to be here."

But after an enumeration of all the inconsistencies and misconceptions into which ignorance will always lead men in such a vital revolution as a change from a licentious idolatry to the faith and practice of the Christian religion, there is still left for us to describe results of a highly gratifying nature, which cannot be contemplated without raising confident anticipations of the time, distant though it must yet be, when Christianity and civilization will be general in the land.

From the schools which have been established in various parts of the country, a number of youths are annually going out, carrying with them, it is true, in many instances, little more than a mechanical acquaintance with the subjects of instruction which had engaged their attention, but with sufficient knowledge to enable them, when increasing years have brought reflection, to improve and turn to advantage the benefits which they have enjoyed. The causes of this great imperfection in their education are various. Unacquainted with the colloquial use of the English language, when they enter the school, associating with companions equally ignorant, and hearing nothing spoken in their families but their native tongue, a knowledge of the sounds which certain formations of the letters of the alphabet represent, without assigning to them any meaning, is all the extent of their information. The English missionary, in like manner, ignorant of the native language, is unable to explain in a manner intelligible to the scholars the meaning of words and sentences, and is obliged to leave the very important task of tuition to native teachers, themselves often imperfectly acquainted with the English language, and still more ignorant of the very difficult art of teaching.

The consequence is, that it is not unusual to meet with lads, who have been at the schools, who will read fluently a difficult passage of English, and who are masters of penmanship, who, at the same time, will not comprehend the meaning of the most ordinary question that may be asked of them, and will be unable to give an answer in English when it is explained. The difference between these lads, and others of a similar age, who have been brought up in the domestic service of a person who is in the habit of speaking English, is very marked. The latter has no hesitation, and readily comprehends whatever may be said. He may be sometimes seen interpreting to his master a communication from the scholar of several years standing, who has not yet learned how to make himself intelligible; nay, we believe that he has been known to dictate a letter for the other to write, who mechanically does so, without knowing the meaning of its contents.

These youths have to complete their education, at best very defective, by seeking the employment of Europeans, and others with whom the English language is in constant and familiar use. Here they learn practically the application of the words, the sound of which had been long familiar to them; and, in a short time, they acquire such an enlargement of comprehension, as enables them to understand what they read, and to explain it to others. There are, doubtless, some who have not to go through this inverted process of instruction: these are the children of parents who speak English, and who are brought up with a knowledge of English and Fantee simultaneously. They have a great advantage over the others, and do not require to wait till they leave school for the comprehension of the meaning of what they have been learning. These carry away with them the knowledge of a few facts, with an aptitude of more readily adding to their number, by a practical acquaintance with the business of life, and intercourse with persons of superior intelligence. Another cause of their imperfect education, is the want of any moral supervision and prudent control out of school-hours, to which may be added irregularity of attendance and a too early departure from school, both consequences of the ignorance of parents, and of their impatient haste to see their children in a position to assist them—an object generally effectually defeated by this very impatience.

We would also with some diffidence advance the opinion, that the course of instruction given is too exclusively of a religious character. While we acknowledge the propriety of religion forming the basis of every system of education, intended for the moral and social advancement of a people, more especially in a country where Pagan idolatry prevails, it is, nevertheless, a well-established fact, that an undivided attention to any particular class of ideas tends to cramp the intellectual faculties, and to limit that generous expansion of the mind which is so essential even to a true relish and an exalted appreciation of the sublime truths of the Gospel.

Another peculiarity is very observable with regard to these youths after they leave school. One would be inclined to suppose, that the ranks of the society would be constantly recruited by numbers of those with whom so much pains had been taken to bestow upon them a religious education ; but so far is this from being the case, that the members who can neither read nor write, greatly exceed those who have been taught to do both. And it is rare for a lad leaving the school, to observe such a correct deportment as will admit him to the honour of membership. It is scarcely doubtful whether this should not be attributed to the rigid severity of their discipline. A gloomy and morose austerity seems to pervade their ministrations. Lugubrious pictures of man's wretchedness are continually set before their imaginations. The sinfulness of youthful levity, and of the gay frivolities which have so many attractions for the young, meets with the sternest reprobation.

The Christian's pilgrimage appears to them a continued series of dark conflicts, of harsh mortifications, of fiery trials, and of dismal horrors. The world is represented as a vale of tears, where wretched man wanders about a vile outcast, until

he sinks with weeping and sorrow into the grave.*
These pictures have no doubt a brighter side;
but such is the predominant character of their
harangues. Their rules of discipline enforce frequent services, a strict and inquisitorial scrutiny,
not only into the life, but into the thoughts of the
heart, a staid solemnity of deportment, an open
exposure of error, and a contumelious dismissal
from their community of every frail member.

However true such representations of man's
character may be, and however efficient such a
system of discipline for separating the chaff from
the wheat, they certainly do not seem best calculated for enticing the young and the giddy within
the fold. They would be more in place among a
nation of Christians, who were relapsing into lukewarmness; or where men, satiated with the vain
cares and pleasures of the world, longed for a
higher degree of spiritual life than could be
enjoyed, amidst intercourse with the worldly.
They would serve admirably the purpose, where
they were sought in true singleness of heart, for

---

* It is not meant to assert, that the calm joys of a
Christian life do not equally form the subject of these
discourses; but these are only understood by the confirmed
Christians, while to the general body Christianity appears a
gloomy and self-denying struggle, which is for ever to place
a grievous restriction upon human enjoyment.

gleaning the pure from the impure; and for a haven to the humble penitent, buffeted by the storms of the world, and seeking amid the sympathy of kindred spirits an outlet for the feelings and emotions of his heart. But to the young African, impatient of restraint, and eager to taste the cup of enjoyment which the effervescent spirit of youth seems to present to him, such dismal pictures and such austere rules, serve no other purpose than to hurry him as far as possible from a missionary; and only when overtaken with disease, or surfeited with excess, will he remember the instruction of his boyhood, and seek for relief in religion.

We cannot avoid thinking that less severity, and less awful pictures of human life, might have the effect of drawing many over to a Christian life at the outset; and when these might be exhibited without any violation of scriptural truth, it is to be regretted that so many should be withheld from assuming the profession and being under the necessity of performing the duties of a Christian. An eloquent and observant historian, in ascribing the effacement of all distinction between Norman and Saxon, and master and slave, in England, to the noiseless operation of moral causes produced by religion, has hazarded the remark that " it may perhaps be doubted whether a purer religion might not have been found a less efficient agent." It would, perhaps, have been nearer the truth to have said, that the national mind of England, at the time referred to, was not in a condition to adopt a purer form of religion ; for religion, in its purity, will always produce proportionate effects upon society. Christianity is undoubtedly suited to man in every stage of his advancement ; but its practical effects upon the life will not be exhibited in the utmost purity where moral degradation has long existed, except among a few rare individuals, whose hearts have been softened by a Divine influence. With the bulk of a people living in "the lust of the flesh, the lust of the eyes, and the pride of life," without a course of previous training, the wrench is too sudden from all their traditionary and immemorial customs, and from all their darling vices and instinctive habits of life, to the pure morality of the Gospel.

Our Saviour's answer to a question put by the Pharisees, would seem to indicate that the heart of man required this previous preparation : " Moses, because of the hardness of your hearts, suffered you to put away your wives ;" and the whole of the Mosaic dispensation, as well as the very gradual and progressive advancement of Christian principles, into what are now the countries of Europe most distinguished for pure Christianity, clearly demonstrate that a long course of years is necessary to mould the mind of a nation for its reception. During these years, there will be much error and misconception in the minds of men, there will be many bright examples of Christian rectitude, and still more mournful instances of human frailty and inconsistency; but truth will finally be written upon the hearts of all, as with a sunbeam, and to mankind raised by its force to the highest degree of moral elevation, strength will be accorded to act consistently with its dictates.

Entertaining the opinions which we have here expressed, we do not think such a rigid system of discipline as the Wesleyans practise, altogether best adapted to ensure great results. We by no means advocate the admission of immoral characters to the full benefits of Christian communion; nor do we blame the missionaries for striving, with a watchful jealousy, to keep their flocks untainted from the vices prevalent in society, and for weeding them as they see occasion; but it is necessary that some means should be adopted to prevent the youths, who are daily coming out from their schools, from giving themselves up to an atheistical vagabondism, neither deterred from vicious courses by the superstitious fears—which are still a check upon their pagan countrymen—nor incited to higher moral attainments by some link connecting them with a Christian community. It were well also, that there were some Christian refuge provided for erring members, where they might hide the shame attached to their expulsion, without losing sight of the duties of religion altogether. If the rules of this Church will not allow it to make some provision of this description, another shepherd is necessary to gather these stray sheep into a Christian fold, where admission to the sympathy of erring sinners like themselves, and to the benevolent ministrations of a Christian teacher, might lead them back from error without suffering the deep humiliation, often too painful for a sensitive mind, of re-appearing at worship in a church where they had lost caste and reputation.

Few of the Christians of England of the thirteenth and fourteenth centuries would stand, we fear, the test of admission to church membership with the Wesleyans of the present day; and yet it is to the men of those times, and to the influence of religion upon their hearts, that the historian has ascribed such a mighty moral and social revolution. May we not then confidently look for similar results from like causes in this country? and ought not this consideration to make us careful not to drive back to paganism and infidelity, men in whose hearts the seeds of religion have been once sown, although they may be choked for a time, as much by the cares and pleasures of the world, as by the barren unfruitfulness of the soil?

Having now adverted to the obstacles which opposed the introduction of Christianity, to some of the most unpromising features which marked its progress, and to what we may have erroneously conceived to be the defects of the system pursued, we will proceed to direct attention to results of a more cheering character. It has been observed above, that many of the most intelligent Christians who first joined the society were now living without its pale. This remark we would be understood to refer to such as had withdrawn from the missionary employment, seduced by the greater temporal benefits which trade held out to them. There still remain, however, in its ranks and employment, a few who have acted with Christian consistency throughout, who, owing to the care taken to qualify them for rendering efficient assistance in extending a knowledge of the Gospel, have arrived at higher theological attainments than any of those who have made shipwreck of their faith.

While trade held out to the latter prospects of greater emolument than they found it possible to

resist, the former chose the better part, and, wisely
contenting themselves with such salaries as their
services to the society should appear to merit, have
risen, step by step, to a high degree of usefulness,
and to an honourable place of moderate competence. These men owe their education almost
entirely to the society. Adopted by it soon after
the arrival of the first missionaries in the country,
and set apart for its service, the greater part of
them were educated at an institution formed at
Accra, chiefly with the view of preparing them for
the ministry. Some of those students have made
an ill-requital for the care and money expended
upon them. Unable to withstand the trading
mania, they ungratefully turned their backs upon
their benefactors soon after the completion of their
education. But some remained faithful, and are
now, as assistant preachers, actively engaged in
propagating the Gospel, giving fair promise, highly
gratifying to the lover of his species, that Western
Africa will, at no distant period, supply a native
band of soldiers of the Cross, qualified, in every
respect, to carry its consecrated standard into the
most distant and darkest abodes of heathen
idolatry.

When we spoke of the offices of the society being
now filled by an inferior class, we had no reference
to this promising band, but to the class-leaders

and exhorters, who, for the most part, are uneducated men, and between whom and the assistant
preachers there is a wide gulf in point of acquirements. These men, converted to Christianity
after having arrived at manhood, and after a youth
passed in idolatrous observances, barbarous customs, and immoral habits, had trials of no ordinary
severity to encounter. The husbands, perhaps, of
several wives, enjoying among their countrymen
offices of distinction in their rude customs, as cap-
tains of companies, attached by long habit to
a certain course of life, they had to cleave to one
wife, to resign positions hitherto the objects of a
fond ambition, to give up cherished practices, and
to bear the jeering taunts, sometimes the enraged
threats, of former companions. The moral courage
capable of such sacrifices could only be derived
from a deep conviction of the unsatisfactory nature
of their pagan rites and customs, and an unshaken
faith in the promises of the Gospel; and to brave
successfully this desperate struggle, a constancy
and firmness was required, which gave to their
character something of the rigid austerity of the
Scotch Covenanters.

It is gratifying to find the names of most of
those men inscribed upon the class-lists for many
years, and to know that they are still maintaining
a consistent life. If they be inferior in point of

knowledge to the others, they equal, if they do not surpass them in zeal. This zeal may possibly sometimes overshoot the mark, and run into wild and extravagant fanaticism; but there can be little doubt that it has its root in a sincere, if somewhat mistaken idea of the duty incumbent upon a Christian. It has always appeared to us, however, among men of this class who have been weaned from idolatrous practices, and who are without education, that their ideas of worship regard the regularity and formality of the act, as constituting a most essential part of their devotion, fully as necessary as the frame of mind which should characterise it. Long accustomed to consider religion as made up of superstitions and ceremonious observances, they have not their minds as yet altogether emancipated from the idea that attention to the external form of worship is of itself a chief constituent part of the Christian's duty, superseding in some instances the necessity of a strict adherence to more essential moral duties which, from early prejudice and the prevailing vices of the community around them, they have been accustomed to regard in a venial light. It is no uncommon thing to find Europeans living in a course of habitual immorality, who would scorn the imputation that they were not Christians, exclaiming against these men, and denying their

claim to this character, because the frailty of our
nature sometimes leads them into the commission
of sin, seemingly forgetting that if they themselves
were judged by the same standard, their own claims
would be discovered to be much more deficient. It
is better surely that the soldier should remain true
to his flag, notwithstanding the occasional loss of a
standard, which a moment of inadvertence or the
overwhelming force of the enemy has occasioned,
than that he should basely throw it away, and seek
an inglorious security where the din of battle will
never reach him more.   In like manner, that
Christian chooses the nobler part, who, true to his
warfare, and with a firm reliance on God, rises
superior to every fall, than he who weakly shrinks
from the struggle, and, alarmed at the sacrifices
which he must make, lives in the neglect of every
Christian ordinance.   With all the imperfections,
then, natural to men under the influence of such
a moral and spiritual revolution, we can see no
reason to withhold from them the merit of acting
sincerely according to the convictions, however
faulty some of their impressions may be, and
notwithstanding that they may not be exempt
from the frailties " that flesh is heir to."

CHAPTER V.

Improved position of women—Effect of Christian marriages
—Difficulties attending the elevation of woman—Sympathy with missionary labour—Hostility of the Fetish
priests—Formation of small Christian bodies— Advantages arising from intercourse with the missionaries in
their journeys through the country—The first missionaries
—Their indiscreet zeal, and its effects—Politic conduct
of Mr. Freeman—Establishment of a good understanding with the chiefs—The progress made by the natives.

Not the least gratifying result of missionary
labour is the increased consideration which it has
obtained for woman. Nothing could be lower
than the state of depression to which purely native
ideas and customs had consigned her, and so
improbable appeared any amelioration of her lot,
that the female mind, familiarised to the destiny of
an unworthy bondage, assumed contentment with
a position which was believed to be her natural
heritage. But another spirit was evoked at the

sound of the Gospel.   No longer constrained to submit to what had hitherto been considered as an inevitable necessity, many of them rebelled against the tyranny to which they had been subjected. They flocked to the chapels to learn the astounding fact, that it was contrary to the law of God for man to have more than one wife.   They returned to their homes, and brooding over this consolatory commandment, were astonished to find themselves regarding with an excess of jealousy which they had never before experienced their co-partners in their husbands' affections.   Curtain lectures became the order of the day ; bickerings were heard in establishments which had been ruled with the quiet despotism of the Grand Turk ; refusals to cohabit with husbands, except upon condition of a general repudiation of his other wives, were of common occurrence ; and such a general fermentation was stirred up in the depths of society, that husbands yielding to the requirements of a Christian life, began to cleave to one wife ; and wives, partly impatient of a divided affection, and partly influenced by a vague idea of Christian duty, in like manner insisted upon a divorce from their pagan polygamist husbands.

We should be too credulous to believe that these separations were invariably the result of a conviction of the sinfulness of polygamy, or of a sincere desire to reform the life. A pretended zeal for religion was, no doubt, in some instances, only a convenient cloak to enable them to get rid of an incumbrance which had become disagreeable; but the faithfulness with which many have fulfilled their marriage engagements, admits no doubt of the conscientious nature of their motives. This fidelity has been much more conspicuous on the part of the wife than the husband, but this fact does not, by any means, imply on her part a higher sense of Christian obligation. The misconceptions which we have noticed as natural to the male Christians, with regard to some views of Christian duty, apply with still greater force to the female, who from the debasing influences of the injurious position assigned to them, had sunk to a lower degree of moral and intellectual degradation. Where a husband is seen faithful to his vows, there can be little doubt of the sincerity of the principle which actuates him; but so many motives concur in imposing this obligation upon the wife, that there can be no want of charity in believing that they have a powerful influence upon her conduct. By her marriage, her position in society has been greatly elevated. She is entitled to the undivided addresses of her husband. He provides more carefully for the wants of his family;

he is a better father to his children, feeds, clothes, and educates them in a respectable manner, and contrary to the native law affecting heathens, leaves them entitled to his property.

With advantages of this description, the institution of Christian marriage became very popular with the sex, apart from religious considerations; and their remarkable fidelity compared with the easy virtue of the polygamist's wife, whether arising from Christian principle or from worldly motives, sufficiently proves their consciousness of their advantages, and their determination to maintain them. The number of these marriages was very considerable, some of them between parties who had been living together as man and wife before the introduction of Christianity, some among the members of the society, who had been cohabiting with several women before their conversion, and who had to repudiate these previous to marriage, and a few among the young men and girls, who had both been educated at the Missionary schools. Of all these classes, the latter is that which holds out the best prospect of happiness, and which approaches nearest to our European ideas of marriage. In both of the former there were mixed up some roots of bitterness. There were children, perhaps, of different mothers, who became to the Christian wife objects of jealousy. There was the knowledge of a former attachment, the embers of which were sometimes supposed to slumber in the heart, ready to burst forth into a new flame. There was the full consciousness of the loose principles of a large proportion of the female community. There was no want of opportunity for, nor allurements to, unfaithful conduct; and there was with all this, perhaps, a want of confidence in the husband's powers of resistance and self-denial.

Where such feelings existed, the shadow of a circumstance capable of suspicion, was sufficient to cause a scene of domestic dissension. The newness of the position of the married wives, so lately raised from degradation, blinded them to the knowledge of their duties, and induced them to exact, as an inalienable and compulsory right, what, if they had known human nature better, they might have made the spontaneous result of dutiful affection. This termagant conduct to men, who had hitherto been accustomed to have their own way in their domestic arrangements, was difficult to brook, and led, we are persuaded, in many instances, to the sin which it was intended to repress. From this and other causes, incident to the state of society, many of these marriages were not always so happy as could be wished; but after making large deductions for backslidings and short-comings, a great proportion is still distinguished for consistent fidelity, and a proper attention to the duties devolving upon them as husbands and fathers. With these and the young couples who have lately been united to the objects of their first affections, marriage is exhibited in its right character. Here Christianity and the domestic affections mutually act and react upon each other. Christianity first formed the link, and domestic felicity, grateful for the boon, finds its most endearing enjoyments, its very existence even, dependent upon cherishing the sacred flame.

The natural result of these Christian marriages has been to give an unity of interest to the husband and wife, which has scarcely any place in the domestic arrangements of the heathen. There the wives rarely reside in the same house with the husband, but come in their turn, or as his whimsical fancy may direct, to provide his food, or to minister to his desires ; attending him, rather with the obedient servility of the slave, than with the affectionate assiduity of a wife. Too much of this lordly superiority still characterizes the conduct of many of the Christian husbands ; but it is fast disappearing, and where it exists, it is as much to be attributed to the abjectness of the female mind, the consequence of early habit and education, as to the domineering conduct of the husband. She, happy in the possession of a husband, who is bound by his marriage vows to remain faithful to her, cares not how she slaves, if she can preserve his affection. She cannot read, and has no mental resources to occupy her attention. Her happiness is bound up in the contentedness of her husband, and the welfare of her children. To secure these, she is satisfied to drudge as for a master, without pretending to the rank of an equal. It is not in the nature of man to practise so much self-denial, as to refuse the acceptance of a superiority, so voluntarily accorded ; and what the woman yields, from a sense of the duty incumbent upon her position, the man comes to regard as his natural right, and only a fitting tribute due to his superiority. The tie of a young family springing up around them, however, and centering their affections upon objects of a common interest, is fast breaking down the barriers between husband and wife, which ages of oppressive severity have rendered natural and instinctive.

It follows, as a necessary consequence from this improvement of the domestic economy of the African, that the condition of the offspring of Christian marriages is widely different from others. The little community of interest called into existence by marriage contracts among the heathen, left the destiny of the children to the fortuitous buffetings of chance. Owing to the peculiarities of the social system, which give to the individual, as has been stated in a former chapter, a property value in the estimation of his family, and which attaches to the maternal side, the father had very frequently nothing to do with his offspring. He did not even regard them as part of his family, in the African sense of the term.

But it is not thus with a Christian family. The vows of baptism impose upon the parents the duty of training up their children in a Christian manner. They are sent to school at an early age. There is a praiseworthy ambition to see them respectably dressed, and fond anticipations are cherished of their becoming useful members of society, in positions to enable them to smoothe the pillow of their own declining age. This instruction is not confined to boys alone. Female schools are in active operation, where numbers of this long-neglected class have been, and are continuing to be, brought up in a knowledge of the the Christian religion, and an acquaintance with every branch of a plain and useful female education.

In the moral elevation of woman, the philanthropist acknowledges the most efficient human engine for the general elevation of a people, and in her debased and abandoned condition, the Christian missionary discovers the most insuperable obstacle to the success of his labours. Nowhere has there been greater necessity for the presence of this agent than in Africa; but the same causes which have produced this necessity, have also occasioned the great difficulty of calling it efficiently into operation. From these causes—namely, the long ages of debasement which gave to the character an instinctive tendency to vicious courses—the peculiarities in the social condition of the people which made the marriage of a daughter a marketable contract, tantamount to rendering female virtue an object of sale, the very lax ideas prevalent in society upon this subject, daily association with friends and relations living in immoral practices, and making them the subject of ordinary conversation, seemingly unconscious of their vileness, the encouragement given to seduction by Europeans, and the fierce impetuosity of passion natural to the children of a tropical sun; from all these, and the numerous modifications of circumstances arising out of them, the missionary found it, at first, a difficulty amounting almost to an impossibility to pilot these frail vessels, beset with so many dangers, into the safe haven of matrimony, without making shipwreck of their virtue.

It is just, however, to acknowledge that this ruin has been as much the result of compulsory measures of bargain-making relations, as of the voluntary act of individuals. This subject is also a fruitful source of sneering animadversion to many who will not see anything good in missionary labour; but with the antagonistic influences which we have enumerated, what else have we a right to expect as a general result? Analogous laws govern the moral and physical world. Can a number of persons in health enter a city infected with the plague, mingle with its diseased inhabitants, eat, and drink, and sleep with them, and yet remain untainted by infection, notwithstanding that there may be in their own systems no predisposing causes? would we be surprized if we were told that the majority were attacked with the malady? and shall we be astonished that those who are exposed to the taint of a moral plague equally virulent in its nature, have not been able to escape its pollution?

To the attentive and candid inquirer after truth,

who duly weighs the influence of the counter-
acting causes which we have enumerated, it will be
matter of satisfaction to learn that there are,
nevertheless, a few exemplary instances of virtuous
integrity, whose escape from the snares with which
they were beset, and whose elevation to the dignity
of Christian matrons, are beginning to give a far
different tone to female morality. It has been
shown, that, however great the dangers and tempta-
tions may be to which the young African is
subjected, they are yet to be withstood by the
influence of Christian principles, and by the
judicious supervision of Christian instructors. The
bridge over the yawning gulf has been crossed.
The pitfalls upon it, numerous as those opened up
to the vision of Mirza, have been avoided, and
finger-posts have been erected by Faith and Love,
to guide future travellers by the same road
past those treacherous snares. Similar difficulties
are never likely to operate again with the same
force, for, in addition to the superior moral tone
which Christian marriages have introduced, the
respect and consideration accorded to educated
married people, and the position of easy competence
which they never fail to attain in society, hold out
inducements which, apart from religious considerations, must exercise a powerful restraint upon the
conduct.

But another cause of far greater weight is now coming into operation. The majority of the female scholars had at first been children of heathen parents, who had been reluctantly persuaded by the missionaries to send them to school. No supervision was exercised over them out of school-hours. On the contrary, they very possibly were accustomed to hear Christian instruction reviled, and practices of an immoral tendency encouraged, by those whom the ties of nature bound them to respect. Now, however, many of the children attending school are the offspring of Christian parents. These, both by precept and example, are bringing them up in new ideas, and subjecting them to those restraints which are necessary to keep them from acquiring bad habits and tastes. With this additional restriction upon the girls, there is every reason to expect more satisfactory results in the time to come, than those which have attended our experience of the past. Every fresh example of Christian constancy on the part of the educated female community will act as a powerful lever to raise others to the same elevation, and the generally improved tone of morality characterising the conduct of those who aspire to European habits, will help to strengthen and confirm those religious bonds, upon which our main dependence must always rest.

Such are a few of the most prominent results of missionary labour. They are limited, it is true, comparatively, to a very small portion of the people. The great masses still cling, although with a less confident grasp, to their idolatrous practices, and their rude and barbarous customs. But, even among these, a great revolution of feeling has taken place. The sentiments of jealous discontent with which they had at first viewed the introduction of the Gospel have died away, and have been replaced by a quiet indifference on the part of the great body of the people, a complacent satisfaction with others, and a hesitating assent to its advantages with many. The indications of an incipient civilization, daily becoming more apparent in the general adoption of the dress and habits of Europeans; the temporal advantages which education is enabling so many to obtain; the possession of those advantages by men who, by their elevation, have acquired extensive influence and have become the central points of attraction to very numerous clans of friends and relations; the natural deference which ignorance pays to a higher degree of intelligence, and the knowledge of the humane and benevolent spirit of Christianity, which idea of its character, though imperfectly understood, is extensively diffused through all classes, have not only overcome all tendency to a hostile opposition, but have prepared the natives for a more general consideration of its claims for acceptance, undeterred by fear of persecution. This amicable feeling is not confined within the narrow compass of the principal towns along the sea-board, where the Europeans reside; but has penetrated into the most distant corners of the extensive territory under British jurisdiction. The Fetish priests are viewing the progress of this state of the public mind with much uneasiness, and are exerting their influence to counteract it, by urging upon the chiefs the necessity of abiding by the customs of their forefathers. They would willingly see the Christians exterminated.

This wide-spread appreciation of the superiority of European civilization, without an admixture of that strong disinclination to keep it far from their doors, which was so general in the commencement, is partly the result of the great advantages derived from the administration of justice by the local government, and the necessary concourse of the chiefs and people of the interior to the towns upon the coast, where they have such frequent opportunities of observing the rapid advance which the natives there are making in every useful art, and partly of the numerous schools and mission stations established throughout the country. To these should also be added the effect which trade has, not only in drawing constant streams of people to the coast, but of sending out into every nook of the interior traffickers with their petty store of merchandize. Many of these are youths who have been educated in the schools. Some of them are in connection with the missionary society. They take up a position in the interior towns where they often reside for months at a time. Their European dress gives them respect in the eyes of the inhabitants, who are eager to know from them all that they can tell of the white men, their customs, habits, and religion.

During this intercourse, new ideas are imparted, important truths sometimes take root in their minds, convictions of their own inferiority and debasement begin to be entertained, and longing desires for their improvement are frequently awakened. But of all these causes, the schools and mission stations are decidedly the most efficient. The sword of justice has a double edge, and cuts in both directions. To one it imparts confidence, to another fear. While it restrains the act, it does not always reach the thought of the heart; it represses crime, but is powerless to instil virtue; and although the arts of peace and moral advancement are beholden to it for protection, and for scope for their full development, yet it teaches no loom to spin, no spade to dig, nor does it enter into the deep recesses of the human breast and bring forth the fruits of righteousness. The civilization owing to the itinerant trader, also, is of a very mixed and doubtful nature. He may be, and frequently is, a worthless and immoral character, and presents to the eyes of the people in the interior, an example unworthy of his education. He may, however, and does often speak of the duty required of a Christian. He can tell of the virtues which he does not practise, and which he has been taught to consider as essential to every good man.

Precepts of this kind, unsupported by example, have seldom much influence, but even from such corrupt sources the knowledge of some truths may be learned, which may give expansion to other minds, and incite them to farther inquiry. With missionary exertion, however, there mixes no injurious alloy. It attacks the vices existing in society; but while it aims at destroying the roots from which they spring, it is careful to sow new seed. The explanation which the missionary makes of his object to the elders of a town, to induce them to consent to the establishment of a school for the education of the young, reveals such a benevolent spirit, and such an absence of all selfish motives, that however slow they may be at first to profit by it, a long course of laborious perseverance seldom fails in gaining them over. A teacher once established, a knowledge of the truths which he has been instructed to communicate, gains its way among the general body of the people.

Faith in the efficacy of their superstitious observances and idolatrous worship is sapped in the minds of a few. They have recourse to the Christian teacher, and are instructed in his creed. They attend his ministrations, and listen, often with awe-struck attention, to his explanation of the Scriptures. One by one, they feel a desire to acknowledge the effect which this teaching is having upon their minds; but shame and fears arising from a variety of causes, beget a restless indecision full of misery. Compelled by the vehemence of the struggle going on in their minds, and unable longer to contend against the convictions which begin to dawn upon them, they request to be admitted to a novitiate. In the process of time a small society is formed. They consent to submit to the discipline necessary for membership, and a watchful vigilance is henceforth kept upon their manner of life. The expulsion from the community of any one persisting in immorality, reveals to the natives generally the wide difference between the frailty of man and the purity of the Gospel.

The sinful practices of professing Christians begat an idea that these were not inconsistent with the Christian faith, and the beautiful precepts which were represented as forming the morality of the Christian, were considered only as something fit to talk about, without any intention of carrying them into practice. It was soon revealed, however, that the weakness of man formed no ground for impugning Christianity. No breach of its morality was allowed to pass without animadversion, and the bare imagination of the acknowledged possibility of attaining such a mastery over the corruptions of our nature, compelled the most bigoted to admit that society could not but derive immense advantages from its consistent practice.

This conviction limited any active spirit of hostility, which still lingered in the minds of some men, to those Fetishmen, and the more elderly of the natives, who were loath to see such a dangerous invasion of their dearly cherished customs. The periodical visits which the missionaries make to these stations, and the constant intercourse between them and the natives generally in their frequent journeyings throughout the country, have the effect of confirming the impressions which have been made, and of diffusing widely a spirit of acquiescent toleration; and thus while the schools in those parts are laying the foundations of a new faith, and of increased knowledge in the education of the young, a variety of causes is at work, habituating the minds of all to the idea of the final triumph of the religion of the white man.

As a proof of the estimation in which European instruction is now beginning to be held, and of the gradually relaxing hold of idolatry, it should be mentioned that it is not uncommon for the superintendent of missions to receive invitations and earnest petitions from distant chiefs to establish schools among their people, and to be entreated by adult persons living in villages, where no branch society exists to visit them, with the view of admitting them for trial, and of instructing them in the duties of Christianity. Until we had paid particular attention to this subject, and had seen to how great an extent this leaven had been infused, it had been, we must confess, always a matter of doubt with us whether the system of widely scattering the mission stations through the country, were as efficient a means of diffusing a knowledge of the Gospel, as the concentrating the whole energies of the society upon one point; thus forming a nucleus which would expand itself in every direction, as soon as the work of conversion had acquired sufficient consistence. But when we reflect how difficult it is to bring the generality of minds to an agreement upon any point, either of faith or practice, how obstinately new doctrines are opposed, that only a small portion in any community will declare themselves until these doctrines have become the creed of the majority; when, moreover, it is seen that the gradual preparation of the mind of a people has been in all countries and ages the necessary forerunner of an entire revolution in religion, we are persuaded that the seed in this country has not been scattered in vain, but that these humble nurseries, where a Christian blossom can scarcely yet be discovered amid the wide waste of heathen barrenness, are the seed-plots, insufficient as they may appear, by which an over-ruling Providence means to raise this hitherto neglected wilderness into a fruitful Eden.

It would be unjust to close this subject, without adverting to the manner in which the missionaries have been enabled to set on foot this silent revolution, and to gain for it the acquiescence of men bigoted in no ordinary degree to their traditionary usages. It has been observed that a very hostile spirit was exhibited on its first promulgation, to be attributed as much to an indiscreet zeal on the part of the missionary, as to the instinctive alarm of a people trembling for the subversion of a system, with an adherence to which their prosperity was supposed to be inseparably bound up. It is with no exaggeration of this feeling that we have remarked, that, but for the protection of the local government, the work would not have been permitted to go on. Even with such countenance and support as it could extend, more than one forcible demonstration has been made to suppress it.

The first missionaries, appalled at the moral waste which the degraded state of the African population presented to their view, and believing it impossible that any race of people, living in such a state of spiritual destitution, would close their ears against a knowledge of the truth, burned with an intemperate enthusiasm approaching to fanaticism to communicate the glad tidings of salvation. In season and out of season, they dinned into unwilling ears loud complaints of their lost and miserable condition. They attacked their idolatrous practices, their social immoralities, and their more innocent conventional usages, and forbade their repetition with such a tone of authority as the possession only of a power to still at once the raging sea or the stormy passions of man could have warranted. With their own experience of the efficacy of religion upon the heart, and under the influence of a strong impulse to impart to others their joy in believing, they seemed credulously to think that the mere announcement of such consolatory truths would at once secure their eager acceptance.

To the jealous comprehension of the African, animadversions upon their customs, conveyed in such loud and objurgatory language, assumed the character of personal abuse; and their pride took offence at what they were inclined to regard as a wanton piece of insult. A too rash interference also with their domestic arrangements, and with the full discretionary power which every head of a family considered himself entitled to exercise over all its members, still farther augmented this spirit of opposition.

Owing to this over-zeal, which looked for a harvest without tillage, and which did not make due allowance for the nature of the soil, much exacerbation of feeling was the consequence. It was not until the management fell into the hands of Mr. Freeman, one who had himself served in the ranks, that a better spirit was evoked. He had

had opportunities of learning, from the experience of his past labours, the necessity of not losing sight of the tendencies of our nature; and he did not think it below the dignity of religion to consult these in his attacks upon their prejudices. He had seen that no dependence could be placed upon the relinquishment of any custom or habit, where the understanding remained unconvinced, and the heart unchanged; and to this important work he directed his best energies. Combining the wisdom of the politician with the active zeal of the missionary, and possessed of an elastic buoyancy of temperament, the result of a firm confidence in the ultimate triumph of the Gospel, he warily reduced the strongholds of superstition, one by one, in the minds of those to whom he gained access; neither arousing hostility by any ill-timed intemperance of assault, nor disconcerted by occasional and temporary failure.

By perseverance in this judicious course, and by cultivating the friendship both of chiefs and people, in his very frequent and extended journeyings through the country, by a kind and courteous affability full of Christian charity, he not only removed all feelings of resentment, but induced them to yield to his guidance in many important particulars. It was seen that a difference of

opinion upon points of belief did not necessarily
form an insurmountable barrier to friendly intercourse, and the Christian missionary thus found
frequent opportunities of inoculating the pagan
chief with new ideas. The natural result of such
an intercourse, will always be the gradual concession of ignorant prejudices to superior intelligence. The chief who would have taken alarm
at a direct attack upon his unchristian practices,
and who would have held aloof with a jealous
suspicion from any one who authoritatively commanded him to abandon them, could see no
danger in an amicable conversation, which was
nevertheless sapping their foundations. Much
credit is therefore due to Mr. Freeman, who
has managed to secure an acquiescent assent for
the free dissemination of Christian truth, which
they feel to be undermining their power, and
to be depriving them of their privileges, which
are best maintained by the ignorance of a
people.

It has often been a question, whether, with
the pecuniary means placed at the disposal of
the Gold Coast Mission, greater results might
not have been expected; and the sums swallowed
up by heavy travelling expenses, have often been
represented as so much money needlessly thrown

away. Christianity, it has been said, needs no extraneous assistance for its diffusion, and should scorn to humour the prejudices of any people. The Christian missionary, like the apostles of old, should provide neither gold, nor silver, nor scrip for his journey. He should humbly wander through the African hamlets, in the firm confidence that the workman will be considered worthy of his hire. Much diversity of opinion will always exist upon a subject of this nature; but our experience leads us to express with confidence, that if this course had been pursued upon the Gold Coast, Christianity as yet would have numbered but few converts. It is doubtful even if the missionary might not have been left to die without any one seeking to provide for his wants. In the Christian, as well as in the pagan world, the surest way to gain friends is not to need them. Nowhere is this truth more evident than in Africa, for, unless an appearance of respectability is maintained, nay, without some indication of the means of being liberal, the European, lay or clerical, will only meet with indifference and neglect.

It has been observed above, that the employment given by the missionaries was a principal cause of their chapels being filled in the commencement. But for the assistance of attractions of this nature, many who are now respectable Christians, would never have been drawn within the reach of Christian teaching at all. Whether, is it better that it should be so, or that barefooted friars should be wandering through the land, exposed to the scoff of the heathen, and without the sympathy of a single convert? Did the power and influence of the Pope give no impetus to the establishment of Christianity in England, apart from its inherent power of disseminating itself? Did the support of Elizabeth's government give no extension to the tenets of the Reformed Church? Teaching is not confined either to the school-room or the pulpit. The active mind of man draws its stores of information from innumerable sources, and is influenced in its adoption of new ideas from innumerable causes. From the cradle to the grave this instruction is in continual progress.

More good may be effected by the journey of a missionary travelling through the interior hamlets, in a manner calculated to secure the respect of the people, by his friendly and familiar intercourse with them, by his example of pure morality, of strict temperance, of Christian charity, as well as by the exhibition of the superior comforts which civilization has placed within his reach, than by the preaching of a thousand homilies. The more frequent the repetition of such visits, the deeper and more lasting will be the impression. Hence the removal of so many prejudices in this country, and hence also the gradual preparation of the minds of men for a new state of things. With such unquestionable proofs of the beneficial results arising from the system which has been adopted, it is impossible to regret that another, less calculated to secure respect for the missionary, and for attracting the natives to his teaching, has not been had recourse to.

Our remarks upon this very important movement now draw to a close. It has been our endeavour to give a faithful representation of what has been passing before our eyes for the last eighteen years, in a spirit of candour and charity. Some of the observations made may appear somewhat deficient in the latter quality; but the prospect of such an imputation has not been able to deter us from giving what we conscientiously believe to be a true picture of missionary labour, and its result upon the Gold Coast. Where there is such an admixture of the elements of progress and civilization with rude and barbarous usages, and where society presents every variety of shade, from the dark and besotted idolater, into whose mind one single ray of knowledge has scarcely penetrated, to the enlightened Christian, already advanced to a moderate standing in the scale of civilized beings, it is difficult in a narrative of this description to avoid the appearance of seeming contradictions and inconsistencies.

The gratifying indications of progress which have to be recounted, and which assume, perhaps, in the eyes of the observer, an exaggerated estimation from contrast with the prevailing ignorance, by which they are surrounded, have a tendency, at one moment, to lead us to believe the condition of the people to be generally much more advanced than we find it ; while, on the other hand, the descriptions which it is necessary to give of the deep moral degradation, and the barbarous and idolatrous practices of the masses, are apt to blind us to the degree of progress which has actually been made.   Only one who has been a witness of this progress can duly estimate its importance.   A passing stranger, who obtains only a casual glimpse of society, and· sees merely its surface, would not hesitate to pronounce it altogether barbarous.

It is, therefore, necessary to caution the reader,

who would wish to carry along with him a just impression of the progress made on the Gold Coast in all its features, not to be so enamoured of its beauties as to overlook the multitude of its defects, nor to fix his attention so exclusively upon its blemishes as to shut his eyes to its merits. He will not err much in comparing it to those land-scapes, where the hand of art loves to introduce, amidst the wilds of nature, some traces of its own fanciful creation, and where may be seen in emu-lous contrast, the wild luxuriance and the stubborn ruggedness of the indigenous plant, and the fair though tender blossoms of the exotic. And when he remembers how many a wilderness has, by patient cultivation, been converted into fruitful corn-fields and smiling vineyards, for the supply of the wants, and as a solace for the cares of man, he will not do wrong in cherishing hopeful anticipations of the time when the natives of the Gold Coast will, by a long process of mental culture, be fully qualified to take their stand among the civilized nations of the world.

CHAPTER VI.

Vague ideas respecting God — Mode of worship — The priests — Evil spirits—Offerings made to them — The immortality of the soul—Worship of the spirits of deceased friends—Slaves killed to attend their master to the next world — Corrupting tendency of idolatry — Prophetic pretensions of the Fetishmen — Tricks and impostures—Children dedicated to the Fetish office from birth—The Great Braffo Fetish—Independent conduct of the Fetishmen—Priestesses—Their infamous conduct —The influence of Fetish upon the African—Decline of the Fetish faith—Its utility as an engine of civil government.

HAVING, in the foregoing part of this work, traced the origin and progress of the connection which has subsisted between the nations of Europe, and the natives of the Gold Coast for a period extending over more than three centuries and a half, and having also placed before the reader a general and cursory view of the existing social condition of the people, with some account of its gradual formation and growth, we shall now direct his attention to their ideas of religion, and some of their superstitious observances, as well as to a more particular account of their domestic economy, without a description of which, the picture would be incomplete. Those subjects, especially the religious practices of the people, may appear to have been of sufficient consequence to entitle them to be incorporated with the account which has been given; but we were unwilling to interrupt the consecutive representation of events by any episodical digression not absolutely required for the perfect comprehension of the narrative, and although we have been obliged to advert occasionally to their Fetish, the expression hitherto has been used more as a general term for a superstitious worship, than as indicating any particular observance requiring explanation.

We shall now, however, attempt to describe the nature of this superstition, which exercises such an illimitable influence over the minds of the masses of the population. An analysis of this description is beset with no ordinary difficulties. We derive little assistance in our investigations from the ideas of the idolaters themselves, which are extremely vague and indefinite, and we are still farther puzzled to discriminate between such impressions, as may be the result of an effort of their own reason, or the consequence of their fears, and such as without the knowledge of the existing generation may have been derived from a more enlightened people, and handed down to them as a portion of the creed of their forefathers.   There is great room to believe that the idea of one great first cause, the Creator of all things, has prevailed among them from time immemorial; for the Fantee words Yankompon derived from " Yankom, " Friend, and " epon," great, and Yammie from " Yeeh" make, and " eme" or " mi " me, by which they designate God, would seem to indicate that the idea of a benevolent Creator was co-eval with the language ; but there can also be little doubt that indefinite as this idea even now is, in their minds, it must have received its confirmation from an intercourse of more than three hundred and fifty years with Europeans, whose acknowledgment of one God must soon have become universally known.   Even before their intercourse with Europeans, it is possible that this great truth might have been disseminated by the Mohammedan population of the interior.   Be this as it may, the natives of the Gold Coast generally acknowledge the existence of a Supreme Being, who made and governs the world, but they cannot be said to worship him.* They sometimes invoke his name, and call upon him to bless those whom they love, and much more frequently to curse those whom they hate, but in either case their invocation amounts simply to an ejaculation, and is not attended by any formal act of worship.

When oppressed with afflictions and overwhelmed by any great calamity, for a release from which they have sacrificed to their idols in vain, we find them resigning themselves submissively to their fate, with the exclamation that " they are in God's hands, and he will do whatever he thinks best." But they neither offer sacrifices to him, nor do they think of seeking by supplication to avert what (if their idols fail them) they seem inclined to regard as their inevitable destiny. To this extent, then, we may regard them as predestinarians, acknowledging one Supreme Governor of the world, who has appointed all things according to his pleasure, and to whom

---

* The manner in which they regard God corresponds exactly with the account given of the Assyrians, whom Shalmaneser transplanted into Samaria, and who, in consequence, became acquainted with the God of the Jews :

" They feared the Lord, and served their own gods. So these nations feared the Lord, and served their graven images."—2 KINGS xvii, 33, 41.

it were in vain for man to appeal with any hope of changing his immutable decrees. They believe, however, that this Supreme Being, in compassion to the human race, has bestowed upon a variety of objects, animate and inanimate, the attributes of Deity, and that he directs every individual man in his choice of his object of worship. This choice once made, the object becomes the " Souman," or idol of the individual. It may be a block, a stone, a tree, a river, a lake, a mountain, a snake, an alligator, a bundle of rags, or whatever the extravagant imagination of the idolater may pitch upon. From the moment that he has made his choice, he has recourse to this god of his in all his troubles. He makes oblations to it of rum and palm wine ; he lays offerings before it of oil and corn ; he sacrifices to it fowls and goats and sheep, and smears it with their blood ; and, as he performs these rites, he prays it to be propitious to him, and to grant him the accomplishment of his petition.

These rites and supplications are directed exclusively to his idol, without any ulterior reference in his mind to the Supreme Being. During their performance, the idolater is sometimes wrought up to a high pitch of excitement, and under the influence of this frenzy, deludes himself with the idea that his idol has mysteriously communicated with him, and granted him an answer to his prayer. He is thus directed, by an extraordinary self-delusion, to the adoption of some ceremonious rite, from the performance of which he expects to obtain the object of his wishes. Nothing can exceed the absurdity of these rites. They bear no reference whatever to the subject of petition as a means to an end. To restore to health a sick child, to shield from danger a friend engaged in some perilous enterprize, or to draw down destruction and death upon an enemy, the idolater may, perhaps, surround his house with a string of withes, hang up some filthy rags to the branches of a tree, or nail a fowl to the ground by means of a stake driven through its body. Whatever wild and extravagant fancy may take possession of his dark and superstitious mind, he believes it to be an inspiration of his senseless block, and to carry it into execution, immediately becomes the subject of a strong religious obligation. Traces of this blind superstition are to be seen on every path, and about the house of every idolater. From the Souman, or idol of individuals, we come to the Boossum of a family or town, which frequently has no material representation. This word literally expresses " take to serve," but it does not so much represent the god of an individual as a family god, or, more universally still, the god of a people. Every family has some god of this description common to all, and every town has one or more also acknowledged by the general body of the people, but a priest or sofoo waits upon this Boossum, and ministers at his altars. As long as men are prosperous, and no extraordinary event occurs to disturb the even tenor of their lives, they are content each to worship his individual Souman; but when calamities overtake them, they distrust the power of their idol to succour them, and their own capacity to interpret aright his inspirations. Under these circumstances, they repair to the sofoo to obtain consolation and relief, from his superior insight into the mysteries by which they are surrounded. An offering is given to him to lay before his god. He explains the nature of the service required, and after a number of absurd ceremonies, arouses his deity to attention, and receives from him an intimation of the observances necessary to obtain his object. These he communicates to the supplicant for priestly comfort, who listens with reverential awe to the injunctions prescribed, and proceeds to carry them into effect with a blind credulity.

In like manner, when the calamity is general, such as a drought, a dearth, a pestilence, or want of success in war, the whole population or their

representatives, with their chiefs and head men,
repair to the chief Boossum to make their offerings
and sacrifice, and to seek, through the intercession
of the priests, a mitigation and a release from
their sufferings. These priests, aware of the necessity of making a deep impression upon such mo-
mentous occasions, surround the whole of their
proceedings with a fearful secrecy and mysterious
solemnity, calculated to awe the minds of the supplicants, and they deliver their oracles in such enigmatical language as may be capable of a double
interpretation. Like the weird sisters in Mac-
beth " they palter in a double sense, and keep the
word of promise to the ear and break it to the trust."

If the observances, which the priests prescribe,
should be performed without any satisfactory result,
it is by no means the fault of the Boossum. It is
immediately attributed to inattention to some religious duty, to the general impiety, perhaps, of the
people, to the neglect of their sacred groves, their
Fetish houses, or a want of a proper respect for the
comfort of the priests themselves. Greater zeal is
urgently recommended, richer offerings are de-
manded, and a renewal of ceremonious observances
prescribed ; and when the calamity, whatever it
may have been, is overpast, the glory belongs to
the Boossum.

This idol worship confines the idolater to no particular idol; as he attributes his prosperity to the protecting care of his Fetish, he will, as long as his prosperity continues, remain steadfast to the worship of that particular Fetish; but when difficulties arise, and he is beset with perplexities, he will range at will, as fancy directs him, to a thousand different objects, and make them the gods of his gross idolatry. The prosperous man is therefore confined in his worship to fewer idols and observances than the unfortunate. The former has faith in the power of his idol, while the latter cannot rest until he has found a relief from his troubles; and hence the multiplication of his idols and of his modes of worship.

Apart from his own Souman, the zealous idolater finds no want of idols in the groves set apart for his worship, in the sea, the rivers, the rocks, and the mountains which surround him. The grander features of nature have a tendency to excite in the Christian's mind emotions of devotional awe and veneration, and at once to raise his thoughts from nature up to nature's God; the mind of the idolater goes not beyond the objects themselves, but their grandeur appals him: they become to him gods, and he seeks to propitiate their favour by an obsequious deportment and vain oblations.

There is one peculiar form, which the Fetish worship of a family about to be separated takes, which deserves to be recorded, as in it we have no external representation of an idol. In view of a separation which will most probably prevent them from ever again worshipping the Boossum, to which they have made their devotions hitherto, they repair to the priest, or sofoo, and having explained their wants, he pounds up some Souman or Fetish substance, and mixes it with water into a drink, which the whole family swallow together. While partaking of this strange communion, the priest declares to them that his Boossum commands that none of this family shall ever after partake of such and such an article of food, naming, perhaps, fowl, mutton, beef, pork, eggs, milk, or anything which he may choose to mention at the time. The Fetish edict, once pronounced against a particular article of food under such circumstances, no one of the family ever tastes it more; and thus we find one who will not taste a bit of chicken, another an egg, a turkey, and so on; and this abstinence from a particular species of food descends to the children, who are under the necessity of observing a similar abstinence. In this case, the parties are supposed to have swallowed their idol, and to have him existing in their own persons, and the abstinence prescribed, forms a continued act of worship.

We do not find that the opinion of a devil, or one great evil spirit, prevails among them. There are modes of expression in use which might lead us to entertain this idea ; but it is found, on more minute investigation, that these are only translated forms of expression suited to meet our European notions, such as " the devil tempted me," " to drive the devil out of town," and so forth, for which the literal Fantee terms express, " an evil spirit tempted me," " to drive all abomination and evil spirits away." But although they do not acknowledge the existence of one superior devil, they believe the world to abound with numbers of evil spirits, who are continually employed about mischief. They deny that they worship these evil spirits ; but if they do not worship them in the proper sense of the term, they have frequently recourse to offerings to bribe them to inaction, or to take their departure.

Sudden illness and diseases, which do not speedily give way to their processes of cure, are attributed to evil spirits, and most of the misfortunes which occur are also put down to the same cause ; and offerings of different descriptions are thrown out upon the paths, with the view of

appeasing these spirits, not to their gods to induce
them to take them away.

Neither do we find that they have any definite
ideas of the immortality of the soul. They are
unanimous in thinking that there is in man a
spirit which survives the body. This spirit is
supposed to remain near the spot, where the body
has been buried. They believe it to have a consciousness of what is going on upon earth, and to
have the power of exercising some influence over
their destiny. Hence they worship the spirits of
deceased friends and relations, and make pilgrim-
ages to their graves, to make oblations and sacrifices to them. But their ideas upon this subject
are as absurd and contradictory as upon every
other point relating to their spiritual concerns.
Unless in the case of the very vilest of malefactors,
they do not associate any idea of punishment in
another world with crimes committed in this;
and the belief that their conduct here will have to
be accounted for hereafter, has no part in their
system.* With regard to a great criminal, we

* Their vague ideas upon this subject may be gathered
from the remark of a criminal under sentence of death. He
had been tried by the assessor and a few of the native
chiefs. The remarks of the former at his trial led the
prisoner to regard him as favourable to his escape; and he

sometimes hear the expression made use of " he will die a second death in the other world;" but this sentiment seems to arise from an impression, that the mere death of the body is not a sufficient punishment for such great crimes, and that a repetition of this, the heaviest calamity which can befal man, ought to be meted out to him, rather than from any conviction that he has to give an account in the world beyond the grave for the crimes which he has committed here. In like manner, they will tell us, that they have no belief in the resurrection of the body; and yet if they are asked where they suppose they go to when they die, they will say that they enter upon a new life in many respects similar to that which they have led here. Acting upon this idea, they are in the habit of burying with the dead a portion of his valuables, in gold and handsome cloths, and placing ready to his hand a flask of rum, his pipe, and tobacco.

Formerly, before the government had obtained

attributed his sentence principally to the native chiefs. On the morning of his execution he said: " I have no fault to find with the white man; he wished to be merciful; but the chiefs are my enemies; and if it be a country to which I am going, I will take care to make them suffer for it, when they come there."

the authority which it now possesses, many of the wives and slaves of the deceased were killed, that they might wait upon him in the country to which he had gone. From preparations of this description, we might be led to infer that they really believed that the deceased had some use for the supplies which they had given him for his journey; but this belief is again glaringly contradicted by the fact, that we find these provident caterers for their deceased relation, sometimes disturbing his bones to rake from them the gold which had been buried with him; thus giving a very satisfactory proof, that whoever else might have been deceived into the belief that gold passed current in the other world, they at least were not the dupes of such a vain idea.

In short, the whole system is full of the most inconsistent contradictions, and cannot stand the test of even an ordinary scrutiny. Had we not divine authority for the awful state of gross and ignorant blindness to which idolatry reduces man in his search after happiness, and for the abominations into which a dark superstition invariably leads him, we should find it difficult to give credit to the evidence of our eyes, for the reality of the impenetrable darkness of the mind, with regard to idolatrous practices which we find existing. It

may be thought by many, that we have here made
the effect and the cause change places ; and that
we should have attributed their idolatry to their
spiritual darkness, and not the excess of this
darkness to idolatry.

But although ignorance is assuredly the mother
of superstition, yet there cannot remain a doubt
in the mind of any one who has attentively watched
the effects of an idolatrous practice, that, upon
all points connected with their worship, the clear
reason and sound common sense, which do not
fail men in the ordinary affairs of life, are entirely
dethroned as soon as the idolater repairs to his
gods. It would appear, as if God by this obvious
phenomenon intended to teach us a lesson of very
weighty import. We may read in the perplexing
doubts, the slavish fears, the barbarous rites, the
cruel sacrifices, the besotted infatuations, and the
filthy bestiality of the idolater's mind, the indignation of the Almighty against idolatry; and
perceive the fearful excesses into which man's
natural constitution will invariably lead him, when
he anchors his hopes on any other than the true
God. The highest degree of intellectual attainment forms no safeguard against the operation of
this universal law. It is exhibited in characters
as unmistakable among the ancient Greeks and

Romans, as among the illiterate people whose religious ideas we have been attempting to explain; and the same law is no less authoritatively vindicated in the career of the Christian, who fails to keep alive his religious impressions, by an abiding trust and dependance upon God.

The account which has been given of the religious ideas of the natives of the Gold Coast, comprehends as nearly as can be discovered the fundamental principles of their faith, if we may apply the term to a principle which involves the contradiction of a facility of belief which no absurdity, how gross soever it may be, can offend, and at the same time a hesitating infidelity which doubts of everything. The articles of their creed which have been laid down, are gathered more from their acts than from any process of reasoning, which have guided the idolaters in the adoption of their system.

At present we can discover nothing but a crowd of ceremonial observances, which we believe to be mechanically performed without much mental participation in the act, without the thoughts of the idolater, in fact, extending beyond the mere act itself. Such a system, where the mind of the idolater alternates between credulity and doubt, and where of course he is ready to yield, for a time, a blind assent to every proposition which his spiritual adviser may think fit to dictate, presents opportunities for deceit and imposture, of which the priests are not slow to avail themselves.

One of the chief characteristics of an ignorant superstition, is a longing desire to remove the veil which conceals the future, and to anticipate events which the Sovereign Ruler of the world has, in great mercy to man, enveloped in darkness. This imprudent curiosity leads the African to have recourse to the Fetishman upon every occasion of difficulty and doubt. The latter, finding so many willing dupes, readily accepts the character of a prophet, with which the fears of the people impel them to invest him. His pretensions rise in proportion to their gullibility, which stops short at no cheat, however monstrous and preposterous it may be. A short experience of applications of this nature, and of the confiding credulity of the people, would soon enable the crafty Fetishman to discover the great influence which these circumstances, in their condition skilfully managed, placed within his reach; and hence, out of the primary articles of their creed, which we have mentioned, has been formed such a system of cunning artifice and methodical imposture, as almost effectually conceals, under the multiplicity of its absurd observances, the groundwork upon which they have been formed.

Without adverting to the many fabulous stories of the origin of this Fetish religion, which are altogether unworthy of a place in a narrative of this description, we will give a short account of the Fetishmen's mode of proceeding, and indicate a few of the tricks by which they contrive to impose upon the multitude. In order to obtain admission into the ranks of the Fetishmen, a course of previous training is considered absolutely necessary. The novice may be either one who voluntarily makes choice of this profession, or he may have been from his birth, devoted to the service of the Fetish. It is not an uncommon practice for mothers, who have been so unfortunate as to lose several children by death, to make a vow to devote the next fruit of their womb to the Fetish, with the view of thus purchasing the favour of her gods for her offspring. The child born under such circumstances is set apart for the Fetish service; and very frequently, on arrival at maturity, fulfils the maternal vow, by becoming a Fetishman. But if his own inclinations should be opposed to this course, an offering to the Fetish is considered sufficient to release him from the consequences of this vow.*

* Leviticus xxvii.

From causes of this description considerable numbers adopt the profession of Fetishmen. It is also customary for a Fetishman to bring up his grandchild to his own calling. He passes over his own children, rightly judging that one of a family at a time is sufficient for all the purposes of a fraudulent livelihood; and he concludes that his grandchild will be ready to carry on the game of deceit by the time that his own age will preclude him from taking a very active part in the Fetish ceremonies.

One of the chief qualifications in the novice is great endurance in dancing, which forms a prominent part of the service. It is from violent dancing to the sound of drums that they look for inspiration. They excite themselves by this exercise into a perfect frenzy, until the Fetish takes possession of them, when they lose all accountability, and toss themselves about wildly, trembling all over, and staggering like a drunken man. In frightful convulsions, with eyes rolling, mouth foaming, and every indication of total unconsciousness of all around them, they perfectly confirm the ignorant belief of their admiring dupes that they are no longer self-possessed, but are under the influence of the Fetish, who leads them whithersoever he will, until nature can no longer endure this tension of her powers, and they sink in a state of complete exhaustion on the ground. The greater the strength of the individual the longer he is able to bear up under his exertions, and the more natural and involuntary he can make these appear, so much the better is he adapted for the Fetish service.

It is generally from qualifications of this description that the aspirants to the higher grades of the order of Fetishmen are chosen. After this, they take lessons from some Fetishman in his craft. He initiates them, however, by slow degrees, taking care to observe well the natural disposition of the novice, and to judge how far he may be trusted with the sacred mysteries. If he unites with the qualifications of a good Fetish dancer, a tenacious memory, a prudent discretion, and inviolable secrecy, he may expect to rise to the highest point of Fetish knowledge; but if he be very deficient in either of these qualifications, but more especially the latter, he will never be allowed to advance in priestcraft. The gross deceits which they are in the constant habit of practising, renders this a wise and very necessary precaution. The foundation of the Fetishman's power being the idle fears and superstition of the people, everything which has a tendency to foster those fears, and to acquire for the priests a character for supernatural knowledge is diligently employed. To this end, they make it their particular study to obtain a knowledge of the history of every family in their district for several generations. The names of their ancestors, with any remarkable event, are carefully preserved in the memories of the Fetish-men, and handed down as a valuable legacy to their successors. By these means, a knowledge of many circumstances concerning individual families is kept alive among the priests, which are unknown to the families themselves, or only vaguely remembered as a very ancient tradition.

This training of the priest, as a necessary consequence, gives him a knowledge of the affairs of his locality, which the curiosity of the African to pry into futurity enables him to turn to good account ; for no sooner has misfortune overtaken a person, than his relations have recourse to the Fetishman to know its issue. Should an individual be sick, they in like manner desire to know the reason. They seldom think of attributing any serious illness to natural causes, such as irregularity of living and a neglect of the means of preserving health ; they look for the true cause in the displeasure of the Fetish, the malice of evil spirits, the incantation of some wizard, or the uneasiness of the spirit of some deceased relation, whose obsequies perhaps have not been properly performed. With these fears of a supernatural agency lurking in their minds, the slightest indication of any cause of this nature intimated by the Fetishman, gains immediate belief, and they deliver themselves up to his guidance with a blind reliance in his perfect acquaintance with the cause of the illness, and in his power to grant relief.

During the interviews which they have with the Fetishman upon the subject, the extraordinary acquaintance which he evinces of all their most secret family concerns, his allusion to past events, and to the circumstances attending the death and funeral of some ancestor, which they may discover to have actually taken place, invest him in their eyes with a knowledge little short of omniscient. This knowledge, be it remarked, he pretends to have learned from his god, after a special consultation upon the subject, attended by offerings and sacrifices, and a great deal of idle mummery, which still further imposes upon his dupes. For the same purpose, they study sleight of hand, conjuring, ventriloquism, and have concealed accomplices to assist them in carrying out their deceits. They generally perform their rights in the recesses of some dark shady grove, apart from the haunts of men, where the solemn stillness which reigns around imparts a character of silent awe to these ceremonies.

However different the result may be from the promises and prognostications of the Fetishman, the faith of the idolater in Fetish generally does not appear to be destroyed. The Fetishman has little difficulty in persuading him that the fault is neither with the Fetish nor with himself, but that the applicant, for some offence which he has committed, is labouring under the displeasure of the gods, who refuse to be appeased unless renewed and richer offerings are made; or it may be, that the cause assigned for the ill success of the means applied, is the disquiet of an ancestor's spirit, who cannot rest, and will not cease troubling his living relations until they have performed certain Fetish ceremonies, and made presents to the Fetish. By such flagrant tricks and excuses, which no extent of ignorance would seem blind enough to accept, but which are nevertheless most credulously assented to, the Fetishmen drive a thriving business, and ruin and enslave thousands by the extravagant and expensive offerings which they demand in the name of the Fetish.

Another, and not the least legitimate source of their influence, is the knowledge which they have acquired of herbs, which has given them, in consequence, a considerable proficiency in the healing art.* In case of sickness, the Fetishman is not content merely with the sacrifices and other ceremonial observances which he enjoins, he makes particular inquiry respecting the nature of the disease; and is able, from his medical experience, to prescribe such medicines as very frequently effect a cure. But while he impresses upon his patients the necessity of attending to his directions regarding the medicines which he gives, he is nevertheless very particular in making them think that it is to the Fetish ceremonies they will owe their recovery.

They still farther manage to extend a high opinion of themselves, and the power of their Fetish, by mutual assistance; and the cunning manner in which they play into each other's hands. They have messengers continually passing from one to another, giving information of what is going on; what parties are likely to come to consult them, on what subject, and generally on every

* The natives of the Gold Coast have no despicable knowledge of the qualities of herbs. A collection of these was, at one time, sent home for analysis; and it was found generally that they possessed some qualities calculated to be of use in alleviating the diseases for which the natives applied them.

matter which is at all likely to be of use to a
brother priest in managing the affair. One Fetishman will acknowledge that his Fetish will not give
any information upon the specific subject; but
commands the person applying to him to go to
another Fetishman, whom he names, and to whom
he has, in the meantime, communicated all the
particulars of the affair.

When application is made to this priest, the
applicant is astonished perhaps to find the Fetishman perfectly conversant with the cause of his
visit, even before he has opened his mouth upon
the subject; and notwithstanding such gross cases
of collusion, the stupid idolater can see nothing in
it but a confirmation of the extraordinary power of
the Fetish. In like manner, when a Fetishman
pays a visit to a town, where he does not ordinarily
reside, his first business is to find out the residence
of the Fetishman of the place, who soon makes
him acquainted with the worldly and spiritual
condition of such of the people as are likely to
seek the ministrations of the stranger; for in cases
of obstinate resistance to Fetish influences, where
the nostrums of one Fetishman have failed, it is
customary to have recourse to another. The crafty
rogues arrange their plans in concert, and proceed
systematically to juggle their deluded dupes to admiration.

But it would be an endless and a wearisome task to follow these cheats through all the various schemes which they have set on foot to consolidate and extend their power. They have only too efficient an ally in the childish and ignorant fears of their countrymen to render this a task of difficulty. We do not find that there is any regular subordination of rank among these priests, except in those cases where more than one minister at the altars of the same Fetish, as among the Braffo Fetishmen at Mankassim, who are regarded as the Fathers of the Fetish of the Fantee country. They have their residence at Mankassim, formerly the head-quarters of the Fantee power, and are looked up to as the most infallible oracles of the country. No fewer than five priests minister at the altars of this Great Fetish. Their numbers enable them to bring into operation a more complicated and better arranged machinery for carrying on their tricks, and their acknowledged superiority over all other Fetishes, and the consequent estimation in which they are held by the general body of Fetishmen in the country, give them advantages in obtaining information, which individual Fetishmen do not always possess. They are seldom consulted in the first instance. It is only when the matter is of moment, or after other Fetishmen have failed to give satisfac-

tion that they are applied to; so that before the
appeal is made to them, they have enjoyed opportunities of making themselves acquainted with the
circumstances of each case, and are fully prepared
to give their answer. But they take care to surround themselves with every concomitant calculated
to inspire awe and fear in the minds of those who
consult them.

Their temple is a deep gloomy recess of the forest,
where the overhanging foliage is so dense, that
scarcely a single ray of light can penetrate it, and
where there is no difficulty in concealing the accomplices of their artifice. Into this den they convey
their dupes blindfolded; and amidst strange unearthly noises, which to the bewildered senses of the
poor terrified idolaters, seem at one time to issue
from the bowels of the earth, and at another to
rush through the air, they make their sacrificial
offerings and invocations to their god, whom they
have come to consult. The confused ubiquity of
the dismal sounds which assail the ears, and make
the hearts of the wretched worshippers quail, is
accounted for by a band of accomplices being stationed around, some in holes underground, and some
among the leafy branches of the tree, and all bellow-
ing out the most hideous and unearthly cries and
groans, which a long practice in this villanous de-

ception has enabled them to utter. When they have sufficiently subdued the minds of their unhappy victims by this discordant concert, and when by violent dancing, and wild and convulsive struggles they have aroused their god to attention, they propound to him the object of their visit. It is not always, however, upon the first application that he will deign a response. This inattention, or rather this contemptuous neglect of the Fetish, is interpreted by the priest in the way most accordant with his own wishes. The applicants, it may be, are told to wait for a more propitious moment, to observe a religious fast, to appease by offerings the evil spirits, or to bestow a richer gratuity upon the priests. It matters little to those hard-hearted men, that they give their dupes long and fruitless journeys in vain. They know that what is obtained with difficulty, is prized proportionably, and they take care that the favours of their Fetish shall not be lightly esteemed. When every penny has been got from their victims, which they can, either by cajolery or by threats, extort, an answer to their petition is resolved upon, and delivered with all those imposing artifices which they so well know how to assume.

But although the Braffo Fetish is considered more powerful, and of a superior order to the other

Fetishes of the country, yet its priests assume no direction over the conduct of other Fetishmen, who each in his particular sphere follows the bent of his own inclinations, and the supposed inspiration of his idols. Different kinds and degrees of power are, however, attributed to different Fetishes. One may be celebrated for his success in exorcism, another for the detection of a thief and the recovery of stolen property, a third for the removal of disease, a fourth for making the barren fruitful and so on. But no jealousy appears to be excited by such preferences. The field for imposture is so extensive, that there is not only a sufficiency of victims for the acknowledged and duly established fraternity to prey upon; but a numerous host of sectaries, simple conjurors, and doctors assume the Fetish character as a very efficient shield for all kinds of roguery, and make large gains out of the credulity of the people.

Neither is priestcraft confined to the male portion of the community. An established order of priestesses, or Fetishwomen, still farther swell the ranks of these religious harpies. Their practice is little different from that of the men, with whom they are associated in most of the religious ceremonies. Their principal sphere of action, however, is in the Fetish processions and dances, which are greatly enlivened by their peculiar costume, their wild gestures, their shrill cries, and their frantic passion. The character of these bedlamites is infamous in the extreme; their life is one continued round of wanton lewdness and debauchery. Under the influence of a superstitious frenzy, and inflamed by the noise of the Fetish drums, and the acclamations of a crowd, they give themselves up wildly to all manner of excesses. But we will not stain our page with farther detail of the enormities of those deluded wretches. Enough has been said to convince the reader, that the miserable state of moral degradation which we have represented as existing among the people cannot have been overdrawn, seeing that such abominable profanity is not only tolerated, but adopted as an essential part of their worship.

The character of the Gold Coast African, the nature of his government, his ideas of justice and its administration, his domestic and his social relations, his crimes and his virtues, are all more or less influenced by, and even formed upon their peculiar superstition. There is scarcely an occurrence of life into which this all-pervading element does not enter. It gives fruitfulness to marriage; it encircles the newly-born babe with its defensive charms; it preserves it from sickness by its votive offerings; it restores it to health by its bleeding sacrifices; it watches over its boyhood by its ceremonial rites; it gives strength and courage to its manhood by its warlike symbols; it tends its declining age with its consecrated potions; it smoothes its dying pillow by its delusive observances; and it purchases a requiem for its disembodied spirit by its copious libations. It fills the fisherman's net; it ripens the husbandman's corn; it gives success to the trader's adventure; it protects the traveller by sea and by land; it accompanies the warrior, and shields him in the battle; it stays the raging pestilence; it bends heaven to its will, and refreshes the earth with rain; it enters the heart of the liar, the thief, and the murderer, and makes the lying tongue to falter, quenches the eye of passion, withholds the covetous hand, and stays the uplifted knife, or it convicts them of their crimes, and reveals them to the world; it even casts its spells over malignant demons, and turns them for good or for ill, according to its pleasure. It might be supposed that a religion with pretensions of this nature could not stand the test of a single week, and that no ingenuity of the Fetishmen could

conceal the multitude of their broken pledges, or
save from exposure the hollow tricks by which
they manage to prop up their tottering faith.
That a race of men, who are by no means
devoid of intelligence, and who upon many other
subjects are perfectly open to reason and to conviction, should continue, time after time, the
dupes of such a childish infatuation, can only be
accounted for by man's innate consciousness of
the helpless nature of his being, and his necessity
for supernatural assistance; his need, in short, for
some faith in things unseen, on which to rest
the anxious burden of his hopes and fears That
they should trust to such a gross superstition
is a humiliating proof of man's natural blindness,
as well as of his vicious and corrupt tendencies.
That they derive some consolation from their faith
is not altogether to be denied ; but it is a fruitless
confidence, ready to be swallowed up in perplexing
doubts upon any untoward occurrence, and only
not altogether lost, because nature is not more
abhorrent of a vacuum, than is the mind of man
of a blank and infidel isolation.

It is very apparent, however, that with a large
number of the people—a number, too, daily
increasing—faith in their Fetish practices is merely

nominal. The more familiar intercourse with Europeans, and the freer interchange of ideas, which have marked the last twenty years of their relations with each other, as well as the effect of missionary teaching, have given an entirely new and vigorous impulse to the native mind, before which the cherished prejudices of ages begin to crumble away. The unsatisfactory nature of their worship is tacitly admitted; its cheerless, deadening influence upon the mind is openly acknowledged; the vile cheats of the Fetishmen are well understood, and observed with a gloomy dissatisfaction; and their punishment by the local government, upon conviction of some glaring imposture, is viewed with a silent and gratified delight. But with all this fermentation going on in the depths of society, the leaven is not sufficiently diffused for any general expression of feeling upon the subject. The time for speaking out has not yet arrived. The gloomy terrors of the Fetish still cast their dark shadows upon minds which acknowledge their thraldom, less from a dread of the spiritual anathemas, which an avowed contempt for, and open renunciation of a belief in Fetish, might bring upon the renegade, than from a well-grounded fear of some vile human agency being employed to satisfy the vengeance of the Fetishmen.

Many, also, among the higher and more intelligent ranks of the natives, who have very little faith in the Fetish, acknowledge its value as an engine of civil government, and give their countenance and support to it accordingly. These men, in our opinion, give strong evidence of their political prudence by this course ; for there cannot be a doubt that, with all its vile impostures and foul abominations, it has a most salutary restraint upon human conduct, and that the removal of this restraint, without the substitution of such a powerful moral agent as Christianity, would at once give loose to the most frightful scenes of a brutal and ferocious anarchy. Considerations of this nature suggest to us the probability of a stage, in the progress of opinion, fraught with dangers to society of no ordinary magnitude, which it will require the whole energies of a government possessed of strong physical powerto avert.

Distrust of Fetish is not necessarily followed by the adoption of the Christian faith. Indeed, it is seen, that at present there is a wide disproportion between the number of Fetish renegades and Christian converts. It is not difficult to anticipate the time, when this disproportion may be increased

to such an alarming extent as will let loose upon
society bands of infidel miscreants, under the restraint of no religious obligation whatever; for
there must be, necessarily, a short period of tran-
sition in the minds of the great body of the
people, full of a wavering uncertainty, which will
take refuge for a while in a lawless infidelity.
Such periods of time in the history of a people
cannot be passed over, even by a strong and
despotic government, without fear and trembling.
For a general revolution of this nature on the
Gold Coast, neither the British local government
or the native authorities are at all prepared.
There may, it is true, be little likelihood of the
near approach of such an event, but a partial
revolution is at present at work, and its effect,
in a minor degree, will be to loosen the bands of
social order. The removal, in part, of the strong
superstitious restraint which has hitherto existed,
will naturally give freer scope to individual action,
and leave men exposed to the wild guidance and
the rash impulse of their own passions, the consequence of which will be the introduction of crimes
almost unknown in the present simple and primitive state of society.

The elements of an extensive social disorganiza-
tion are now fermenting in its depths, and give

token, by a grumbling discontent and an agitated alarm on the part of the higher classes, and by an uneasy restiveness, and a partial disregard of their masters on the part of the slaves, of the breaking up of many of those fetters, which time and the right of might had rivetted upon the bodies and minds of the people. The powerful chief, and the wealthy slave-owner alike hold the reins of authority with a less confident grasp ; and even the cunning Fetishman feels that he must lower his pretensions, and moderate his extortions if he would not see his victim drag him into a court of justice. These are certain indications of a new and more enlarged class of ideas being generally diffused throughout society, and are the forerunners of change. The danger is, that the first taste of emancipation, however circumscribed, may be so sweet, that an ignorant impatience may hurry men into excesses, destructive of all order. It is on this account that government, during the progress of a revolutionary spirit of the kind, should strengthen themselves for the occasion, as much by a skilful and liberal direction of this spirit to its legitimate objects by lawful means, as by a bold and uncompromising resistance and repression of every illegal act. On this account, also, it is that a renunciation of Fetish, by the general mass of the people, is by no means desirable, unless it should be supplanted by Christianity with its peaceable fruits. The local government upon the Gold Coast must have the candour to acknowledge its obligations to Fetish, as a police agent. Without this powerful ally, it would have been found impossible to maintain that order, which has characterized the country during the last twenty years, with the physical force of the government. The extraordinary security afforded to property in the most remote districts, the great safety with which packages of gold of great value are transmitted by single messengers for hundreds of miles, and the facility with which lost or stolen property is generally recovered, have excited the astonishment of Europeans newly arrived in the country.

But while much of this excellent police has been due to the energetic measures of the local government, the superstitious fears exercised over the minds of the people by the Fetish, have also had a powerful controlling influence which ought not to be lost sight of. During these years, so little complicated were the relations of society, so unvarying its usages, so great the subordination of its different ranks, and so rare the commission of crime, that a few magistrates, assisted by a small body of police, were found perfectly sufficient for all the purposes of good order. But daily experience now shows that this system is no longer adequate to the present circumstances of the people. The government has now to exercise a more extensive and subdivided watchfulness over the masses. The obedience which the slave formerly unhesitatingly yielded to his master, the dependent and feudal retainer to his chief, and the general body of the people to their Fetish observances and obligations, concentrated the controlling power within such a narrow compass, and, at the same time, maintained this power in such perfect efficiency, that the government had only to keep a watchful eye over these directing influences, in order to secure its object, the general order and peace of the country.

If these agents had been content not to abuse their authority, the same system would no doubt have been continued in all its original efficiency to the present time; but the cause of social progress would not have advanced with the rapidity which their abuse of their privileges has occasioned. The oppressions of masters, the tyranny of chiefs, and the extortions of the Fetishman having exposed them, on various occasions, to punishment, their authority fell into contempt; and hence arises the necessity of the government to substitute new checks, to replace those restraints, which are daily losing some portion of their efficiency, and will soon become obsolete. Happy will it be for the Gold Coast population, if the government has the wisdom and the power to carry them peaceably through such a moral and social revolution. Their very docile disposition is our surest ground of hope; but we must take care to direct this disposition to its legitimate objects, by fortifying those minds which are throwing off the yoke of the Fetish with a purer religion.

Intelligent natives, who have the penetration to see the tendency of Christian instruction, and the other civilizing influences in active operation, tremble for the consequences of a struggle between the two great principles of civilization and barbarism, which are beginning to form the people into distinct camps. They see the ancient landmarks of society disappearing, and attribute much of it to the roguery of the Fetishmen, who, by their extortions, have alienated the allegiance of the Fetish-worshippers, and have branded the whole system with the character of imposture. They look for the preservation of order to the reformation of the Fetishmen, and would gladly see some Luther arise among their ranks, to sweep away the abominations which have been heaped

upon the primitive simplicity of their worship.
They feel no enmity to Christianity; for they see
that it inculcates peace, order, and a higher regard
for the rights of individuals, and for the general
good. But they have no faith in its becoming
the rule of life of the multitude, who can only,
they think, be kept in check by the power of the
Fetish.

There are a few, again, who would wish to see
the Christians persecuted and utterly exterminated.
They have no favour for education, and cannot
see the gradual progress of civilization without a
wish to crush it entirely. These are not so much
bigoted zealots, as alarmed for an invasion of
many of their privileges, which the Fetish superstition enables them to secure. The Fetishmen
themselves, with the short-sighted blindness
natural to a very long practice of low cunning,
though aware of the necessity, do not seem to
yield much of their pretensions. It appears impossible to shake their faith in the credulity of
their dupes. This, indeed, is not to be wondered
at, when we find their own minds, in spite of
their knowledge of the infamous impositions to
which they have recourse, deeply imbued with a
superstitious dread of the Fetish. The very men
who have spent a lifetime in obvious and pal-

pable trickery, seek relief in the same mummeries,
in their own misfortunes.   Can there be a better
evidence of the doubting principles of a creed like
this than such a fact ?   Weak indeed must be the
confidence, cold the emotions, and spiritless the
consolations, derived from a source known to be
based on lying cheats.   The knowledge of this
fact, added to a consideration of the foregoing
details, will afford us, perhaps, the best clue to a
proper definition of Fetish, and the hold which it
occupies on their minds.   Dr. Beecham traces the
polytheism of the natives to the following tradition :

"It is believed, that in the beginning of the
world, God having created three white and three
black men, with an equal number of women of
each colour, resolved, in order that they might
be left without complaint, to allow them to fix
their own destiny, by giving them the choice of
good and evil.   A large box or calabash was, in
consequence, placed upon the ground, together with
a sealed paper or letter.   The black men had the
first choice, who took the calabash, expecting that
it contained all that was desirable ; but upon opening it, they found only a piece of gold, some iron,
and several other metals, of which they did not
know the use.   The white men opened the paper
or letter, and it told them everything.

"All this is supposed to have happened in Africa, in which country it is believed God left the blacks, with the choice which their avarice had prompted them to make, under the care of subordinate or inferior deities; but conducted the whites to the water-side, where he communicated with them every night, and taught them to build a small vessel, which carried them to another country; from whence, after a long period, they returned with various kinds of merchandize, to barter with the blacks, whose perverse choice of gold, in preference to the knowledge of letters, had doomed them to inferiority."

Dr. Beecham adds : "Is this notion of the judicial degradation of the blacks traceable to the curse pronounced upon Ham? And is this again confounded with the result of man's probation in Paradise? These are interesting questions; but however they may be decided, it is certain that in this tradition is to be found the source of those superstitions which enthral millions of the negro race."

We suspect that this tradition, which is correctly given, does not date its origin further back than the period of the first acquaintance of the natives with the Europeans. It seems to us rather a theory formed from the observation of the circumstances of their respective conditions, than the fundamental source of their superstitions, which must have existed before the tradition, and which are to be accounted for, simply by a reference to man's natural constitution. Unassisted reason has never yet, we believe, led man to entertain just conceptions of the being and attributes of the true God. The speculations of Plato and of Socrates, founded upon an enlightened contemplation of nature, approach nearest to the truth; but it is manifest that notwithstanding the clear evidences of power, harmony, and unity, which they observed in creation, their ideas of God were vague and indefinite, and only amounted to a plausible conjecture, not to a belief on which their minds could securely rest.

Heathen nations generally have fallen far short of the conclusions to which these great logicians attained. They have been guided more by their spiritual instincts than by reason, and have never arrived at the idea of one God, however much the forms of expression might lead us to think so. The operation of our spiritual instincts is as powerful, though less discriminating than our physical instincts. The feeling of hunger impresses man with the belief that there is something provided in nature to appease it, and would lead him to seek to remedy his want, even if he were ignorant of the nature of food. If he is thirsty, he feels that there must be somewhere a remedy for this also. If he is sick, still instinct leads him to look for relief amidst nature's stores. In seeking to gratify those instincts, he might, it is true, take poison for nourishment, and apply remedies which would aggravate his disorder, but the instinct would still remain, and lead him to a discovery of the objects in nature calculated to satisfy it. In like manner, his spiritual instincts urge him to look abroad through nature for relief. He feels that for them also some provision has been made ; but he is directed in his search by no certain test, and hence the multiplicity of his objects of worship.

Guided by this impulse, the African has stumbled into a belief in a mighty, supernatural, and intelligent influence, pervading all created things, but dormant and unconcerned about the affairs of men, until by an act of faith and worship, the idolater has constituted its special abode for the time, aroused its attention, and purchased its services, which may be made either subservient for a blessing, or instrumental for a curse. He is directed in his particular manner of worship at all times by his own fluctuating doubts and fears, for he has no assurance of the form of worship and rites most acceptable to his idol, hence his multiplicity of superstitious observances, his wavering doubts of their efficacy, and the influence of the Fetishmen, who pretend to frequent and familiar communication with this supernatural intelligence. Its hold upon the minds of those under its influence is unbounded; for the faith of innumerable worshippers having given a local habitation to this intelligence upon every hand, wherever their extravagant fancies may have directed, and their prayers and sacrifices being supposed to have purchased a fulfilment of their behests, an endless variety of emanations, in conformity with the will of the supplicants, is believed to be continually proceeding from these idols, which have become, by an act of worship, the consecrated abode of a living intelligence; hence a perplexed dread in the mind of the idolater, of becoming at any moment, through misfortune or ignorance, or in answer to the particular prayers offered to an idol, the unhappy butt against whom those subtle influences may direct their invisible attacks ; hence also the necessity for countervailing observances, charms, and spells, to preserve him from such attacks, or to render them abortive. In his mind, and to compare spiritual with material things, the spiritual world may be likened to the firmament, with its galaxy of stars, which from its otherwise dark surface shoot innumerable scintillating rays, each according to its magnitude, and from their combined influence diffuse a light which pervades space. In like manner, the idolater appears to be subjected to the eyes of an all-pervading intelligence, which surrounds him with an atmosphere of mysterious combinations, deeply affecting his destiny.

When contemplating the African, under the influence of purely superstitious emotions, we have never been able to remove from our mind the idea that he regarded the material world as a breathing animated mass, watching him from a countless number of sleepless eyes, which kept him under continual alarm and restraint. Such appears to us the nature of the superstition known to Europeans under the name of Fetish. If the account which has been given should fail to leave upon the mind of the reader a clear and intelligible comprehension of the subject, we must plead the impossibility of bringing light out of darkness, or of escaping entirely from its inherent mystification. It is enough for us, if, from a higher vantage-ground than the idolaters themselves possess, we have been able to throw upon their benighted superstitions a glimmering from our own rush-light, which may direct other minds more deeply versed in the mysterious operations of the human heart, to a lucid solution of its strange and unaccountable vagaries.

CHAPTER VII.

We have now taken a general view of the people
and of their superstitious belief, and would desire
to place before the reader some account of their
ordinary habits of life ; but this we find impossible,
without being obliged to recur, at every step, to
their Fetish practices, so much are they incorporated with the every-day occupations and pleasures
of the African. It is to be lamented that the
heathen should, in this respect, exhibit a more

constant, steadfast, and pious dependence upon his idols than the Christian does upon God, and that man, relieved from his superstitious fears, should so often subside into indifference with but few indications of a reverential and grateful heart. It is rare for them to omit, morning and evening, to make some oblation to their Fetish, or to pay their homage when they eat or drink. They undertake nothing even of ordinary importance, without raising their thoughts to an unseen intelligence, and propitiating it by some observance, while humble thank-offerings invariably attend its successful issue. If they were content to confine themselves to this humble and thankful dependence, we might regret their ignorance of the true object of worship, while we applauded the spirit which dictated it ; but, unfortunately, their belief in a multiplicity of deities leads to the idea of a variety of discordant attributes, which render necessary a multitude of observances. Their vague ideas of a future state of rewards and punishments, amounting practically to a disbelief of such a state, limit the operation of their spiritual instincts chiefly to the circumstances of their present existence ; which are all more or less influenced by them.

War is never undertaken by kings or states without consulting the national deities. The Fe-

tishmen "go up to inquire"* of their idols, after
sacrifice being made, and unless the response be
propitious, they will not engage in it. Renewed
offerings and sacrifices are made to obtain the
favour and assistance of their gods, and a promise of
success. This once secured, they meet their enemies with confidence, relying as much upon the
protection of their gods as their own bravery.
After victory, the glory of which belongs to the
Fetish, they propitiate a continuance of his favour
by sacrificing many of the prisoners taken in war.
These are considered especially grateful to their
tutelary gods. This idea seems to arise from the
belief that, in international wars, the protecting
deities of one nation are contending against those
of the other, and are equally interested in the result
of the warfare with the mortal combatants.

Fetishmen accompany the warriors to the field,†
and urge them to deeds of daring and bravery by
the promise of supernatural aid, and by the invo-

* Has this practice, which has been so generally followed
by the pagans, been derived from the Mosaic system of
appeal to the Deity ; or was the latter adopted out of regard
to the natural constitution of man, and consequently universal ? We believe the latter conjecture to be the true
solution.

† This custom of the priests attending the army to the
field is also of a very ancient date.—*Vide* Numbers xxxi, 6.

cations which they never cease to make. Their captive enemies are consequently regarded as the enemies of the victor's Fetish, and no sacrifice is so acceptable as their blood. Hence those wholesale slaughters of vanquished enemies which attend the victories of the kings of Ashantee and Dahomey, proceed not so much from the blood-thirsty disposition of the African, as from a religious sense of duty to their gods. Want of success is sometimes, but not always attributed to the inferiority of the gods of the vanquished. The Fetishmen do not easily give up their defence, and frequently manage to convince the conquered that their failure is owing to their displeasure, for the omission of some observances, for national impiety, or for inattention to prescribed ceremonies. After the conquest of Fantee by Sai Tootoo Quamino in 1807, the faith of the Fantees was considerably shaken in the Braffo Fetish Mankassim, which, up to this time, enjoyed an extraordinary share of national favour. The Fetishmen, however, had always been averse to the war, and they now took occasion of this known aversion to excuse their defeat, and the worshippers were soon brought back to its altars. It is worthy of remark, that although the Ashantees destroyed Mankassim, they had respect to the Fetish grove in its immediate neighbourhood.

Treaties of peace and amity are also entered into with Fetish ceremonies. Having witnessed several of this description at Appollonia, we will here give a short description of them.

After the capture of the King of Appollonia, deputies arrived from neighbouring states to enter into a treaty of peace, and among others a party of Assinees. They assembled under a large tree in the centre of the town, and seated themselves in two semi-circles, the Appollonians on one hand, and the Assinees on the other. They then discussed the different articles of the treaty about to be concluded, and evinced the greatest anxiety to obtain a very clear and distinct understanding on each item. Twenty of the Appollonian head men then came a little in advance of their party, and sat down upon the ground ; the Assinees carefully examining their persons, and removing from them their knives and ornaments, lest they should intercept the virtue of the Fetish. They next addressed them, repeating the nature of the engagement, entering minutely into the different terms of the treaty. When these were all agreed to, which was not done without sundry explanations of the light in which the Appollonians understood them, and which showed that faith was actually placed in the power of the Fetish by their anxious care not to compromise themselves by an imperfect comprehension of their engagements, the Fetishman, or priest, of the Assinees produced a shell filled with some odious black compound, which he mixed and stirred with a piece of stick. He then stood up and spread his arms over the Appollonians, and evoked the vengeance of the Fetish if they should prove faithless to the treaty. After his invocation, he was about to administer the nauseous mixture, when the Appollonians called out loudly to the Assinees first to take a little of it into the mouth of a few of themselves to convince them that there was no poison. This being done, they smeared the tongues of the Appollonians with the stuff in the shell, and waved it over the other Appollonians standing about, to bring them all under the binding of the oath. A similar process was then gone through by the Appollonians administering Fetish to the Assinees, and the ceremony was at an end. It is not necessarily confined to one set form. Upon another occasion we saw green leaves mixed in a calabash with a dark liquid, used as the sacred draught. The head men took a little of it into their mouths, and the remainder was sprinkled over the multitude standing round.†

* Here, again, we would appear to have fallen in with an ancient observance—Exodus xxiv, 8. " And Moses took

In their judicial proceedings, also, the Fetish element predominates. We have already adverted to the Edum draught, which is administered to discover guilt; many other ordeals are also had recourse to, for as the constitution of the African mind leads the people to attribute misfortune and death to supernatural causes, they are constantly employing Fetish practices to discover the guilty. An instance of this description occurred near Anamaboe, about sixteen years ago, which will serve as an illustration. At the village of Aggrey-fooah, a man of the name of Yow Nacoon, was seized with a lingering illness which seemed to set at defiance all the nostrums of the doctors and Fetishmen. Eggs had been bespattered about the door-posts, strings and rags had been hung up to the branches of his Fetish-tree in the yard, the empty bottle suspended over the door-way had been appealed to, charms had been tied about his person, stones encircled with rags and feathers, bread besmeared with palm-oil, yams nailed to the ground with stakes, and white fowls sacrificed, all to appease the evil spirit, and in vain—he died.

The Abrah Fetish was consulted, with the view

the blood and sprinkled it on the people, and said, Behold the blood of the covenant, which the Lord hath made with you respecting all these words."

of discovering the author of his death. His family were ordered to appeal to the dead man, which was done in the following manner. The inhabitants of Aggreyfooah were assembled upon a spot near the village, seating themselves in a circle according to their different wards or divisions. In the centre of this circle a stake was set up, covered with leaves and branches. The corpse was then brought out on a shell, and was carried on the heads of bearers. The Fetish drums kept beating all the time, as the bearers danced round the circle. At last they came to a dead halt before one of the divisions of the town. They appeared to strain every muscle and nerve to go forward, but no sooner had they extended a foot than they were pulled back by some invisible power. On every side, the same controling influence restrained them, and there they remained, struggling and pulling against the spirit, until overcome by their exertions they sunk under the body to the ground. The other divisions immediately rose up, and declared the murderer of Yow Nacoon to be one of the division before which the dead man's spirit had compelled the bearers to halt.

This proceeding had been carried on amidst the noise of the Fetish drums accompanied by dancing, and amidst the fears of the assembled divisions lest the lot should fall upon them. They now carried the body to the village, and passed round in the same manner all the houses of the guilty division. The bearers at last halted involuntarily before one of the houses, where of course the murderer was declared to be. All the inmates of the house were now subjected to a similar ordeal, and the spirit compelled the bearers to fall at the feet of an old man named Cogo Fee, who was unanimously pronounced a wizard.* He was drowned at night by the head men of the village; and the knowledge of this circumstance did not come to the ears of the English authorities until fourteen years afterwards, when all the circumstances were fully confessed, and the perpetrators condemned to imprisonment for a number of years. Of course it had been previously arranged who the victims of this ordeal should be, and the bearers had been instructed to act accordingly.

Witchcraft is a crime which entails by the African laws not only death upon the witch or wizard, but death or bondage upon their relations also. It is chiefly discovered by the Fetishmen, who suit

---

* We have, in the Old Testament, a trial by lot, of a similar description, descending from tribes to families and individuals, although we have no account of the process.— *Vide* Joshua vii, 16, 17, 18, 19.

their own purposes in denouncing the guilty. If sudden illness or death should overtake a person, who had chanced to have a quarrel with another, this other is supposed to have bewitched him, and rarely escapes punishment. Appeals are also made to the Fetish by persons accused of witchcraft to be relieved from the false imputation, and if declared innocent, heavy penalties are decreed against the accuser.

Persons are frequently charged with having in their possession dangerous Fetishes, which bring calamities upon their neighbours. A curious case of this description was brought under the author's notice. A native of Akim summoned a Fetish-woman before him, whom he accused of having caused the death of a number of his relations. His story was, that this woman and her family were slaves of an Akim chief, who had died. The Fetish was consulted as to the cause of his death, and pronounced it to be owing to this woman's bad Fetish. She was seized in consequence, and was about to be put to death, when she contrived to escape, carrying her Fetish with her. Some time afterwards, she was discovered in another part of the country by a member of the Akim chief's family, who assaulted and beat her, and knocked her Fetish, which she was carrying, off her head. Enraged at this treatment, the woman poured out a libation of rum before her Fetish, and invoked its wrath upon the aggressor's family. Since that time, six members of his family had died, and a seventh was labouring under a mortal disease at the time he made his complaint. These misfortunes he attributed to the woman's curse, and he pleaded that she ought to be delivered up to him in the first place as his slave, and in the next, that he might deprive her of her Fetish. Nothing could exceed the earnestness with which he pleaded his cause, and the superstitious terrors under which he was labouring were evidenced in the tremor of his accents, and in the heavy drops of perspiration which rained down from his face.

The woman acknowledged that she was his slave, and that her daughter and four children were still in bondage at his house at Akim. It was six years since she escaped from that country flying for her life. She admitted having invoked her Fetish to curse her master's house in the heat of her passion ; but it was a long time ago. She did not, however, appear to deny that she believed the misfortunes of his house to be owing to the anger of her Fetish. Indeed, there was visible in her deportment an air of satisfied triumph in the power of it. She prayed with great earnestness, that she

might not be deprived of it, as she obtained her
living by its assistance. It was represented to her,
that she had been at least guilty of the murder of
the heart, as she had faith in the efficacy of her
Fetish when she invoked the curse upon her master; and that while he as well as herself entertained this belief, it was not proper that she
should be allowed to keep such a dangerous
Fetish. It is very difficult to deal with such cases
as these, as it is utterly impossible to reason with
them upon the subject.

In the present case, it was arranged that the
Fetish should be taken from the woman, and that
she should be free from her master. But it was
not sufficient to deprive her of the Fetish alone;
the Akim man wished it to be delivered to him,
that he might carry it back to his country, and
appease its wrath, by worshipping it and sacrificing
to it, in order that the curse might be removed.
Without it, in fact, he considered himself lost, as
he believed that unless he had the opportunity of
appeasing it, he himself and all his family would
inevitably perish. Advantage was taken of this
feeling to obtain the freedom of the woman's
family, and the Fetish was to be delivered up to
him, only upon their being immediately restored
to the woman free. He eagerly consented to this

arrangement, but the woman seemed to prefer the Fetish to her children, and it was only by compulsion that she relinquished it. Her daughter and her four grand-children were handed over to her with certificates of freedom, and the Fetish was given to the Akim man.

Some idea may be formed of the effect of this superstition upon their minds, when it induced this man to part with five slaves and to travel a distance of more than a hundred miles to get possession of the Fetish, and led the woman to esteem it of more value than her children. It was brought into court carefully covered over with a white cloth, which, on being removed, gave to view a brass pan containing a lump of clay with parrot's feathers stuck in it.

With this dread god, the poor man went away greatly relieved in mind ; but the awe-struck manner in which he placed it on his servant's head showed with what a superstitious fear he handled it ; while the woman, now reconciled to the sacrifice which she had made, consoled herself with the belief that Yaukumpon* would direct her in the selection of a new Fetish. It may be thought absurd in an European to entertain such cases at all, but unless we were to hear them, they would

* God.

settle the matter in their own way by killing the whole family. Neither would it have been sufficient to destroy the Fetish, as their superstitious terrors would still have haunted them, and induced them to have recourse to new cruelties.

The Fetishmen are applied to almost in every concern of life, to detect thefts, adultery, and the perpetrators of every crime against society, as well as to avert misfortune, to procure a blessing, and to reveal future events. Applicants for priestly aid carry with them presents to the Fetishmen,* and often impoverish and enslave themselves in their eagerness to secure their services. Such credulity exists among the people, that the most barefaced impostures frequently pass unnoticed and unredressed, and it is only when serious calamities overtake them, through this agency, that a magistrate is applied to.

We will here relate a case of conjuring which was brought under our notice some time ago. A woman belonging to Cormantine, summoned a Fetishman of Dixcove to answer the charge of having falsely accused her son of theft, on account

---

* This custom of carrying presents to the Fetishmen appears similar to the practice followed in ancient times, upon application made to the prophets—Saul to Samuel, Naoma to Elisha, Benhadad to Elisha, &c., &c.

of which she herself and her children had been sold to make restitution for the property alleged to have been stolen, and to pay the services of the Fetishman. It appeared that a neighbour of this woman had lost his *foutra,* or purse, said to contain a great deal of gold. He had recourse to the Dixcove Fetishman to discover the thief, which he pretended to do by means of his conjuring, and fixed the guilt upon the son of the woman; and afterwards forced her to make good the loss.

This Fetishman appeared in court dressed in a white Moorish robe, curiously bound round his waist with a girdle. On his head was a mitre-shaped hat of fine matting. A large string of white and black beads encircled his neck, and hung down over his breast. Small bells were attached to his dress, and iron castanets were round his ankles, and these made a ringing noise on every movement of his person.*

He was a strong young man, with an air of conscious importance in every look and gesture. He admitted at once that he had detected the thief, and had caused him and his mother's family to be sold, to make good the loss. The money gained

* The dress of a head Fetishman, whom we have seen at Pram Pram, appeared something like a caricature of the High Priest's robes.—*Vide* Exodus xxix.

by their sale had been paid to the party the purse was stolen from, after a deduction of five pounds for his own trouble. He acknowledged that he had no evidence whatever of the boy's guilt, nor even of the existence of the purse alleged to be stolen, except such as he had obtained by conjuring. He was desired to show how he proceeded in this matter; and he coolly took out from a pouch which he carried at his side six leathern thongs, and threw them upon the floor, saying, these had given him the information. He was asked in what manner, and he proceeded to twist the thongs, and to place the ends of them in a confused heap, and having done so, said that they were now speaking to him, and still telling him that the boy was the thief. Being asked if he thought we could hear what the thongs were saying, he answered that we might, if we would look at them in the right way; upon which, we pretended to examine them curiously, and then said, that we now understood them, but that they did not speak the same language to us as to him. He asked what they said, and was told that they commanded him, the Fetishman, to be immediately tied up and flogged with them, as a cheat and an impostor.

This sentence, which appeared to give great satisfaction to a crowd of people assembled in court, was carried into effect, and the Fetishman received two dozen lashes with his oracular thongs. The woman and her children were moreover redeemed, the Fetishman and his accomplices having been compelled to make restitution. After this, he decamped from that part of the country as speedily as possible, much crest-fallen, but only, we believe, to renew his cheats in another district, which the report of his treatment had not reached. In cases of this description, they may possibly have some grounds of suspicion, but frequently not, and they are directed to their victims by their utter helplessness.

In the case of suspicion of adultery, the woman is carried before the Fetishman, and required to prove her innocence by an ordeal not dissimilar to that required by the Levitical law.* The bitter draught which she is given to drink is supposed to have the power of bursting her belly in the event of guilt, and the terror of such an ordeal frequently leads to confession. Conviction of this crime with a king's wife is followed by death; and the original law appears to have contemplated this punishment generally, but pecuniary compensation is now the practice generally of the country.

We find the natives keeping general feasts at stated times, which are likewise a part of their

* Numbers xxxi, 11.

religion, and are attended by a great variety of ceremonious observances. The priests compute the time of their approach, and summon the people to prepare themselves to observe them. National sacrifices and offerings of the first-fruits of harvest are invariably made, before the kings or people presume to make use of the new crop; and in addition to this general solemnity, every individual makes separate offerings for himself and family upon the day that they first eat of it. About the same time that this ceremony is observed, it is customary for all the males to parade themselves through their villages, and to clear the paths leading to their Fetish groves.* During these processions, they sing aloud the praises of the deities of the country.

They are also in the habit of propitiating the gods of the sea to give them abundance of fish in seasons of scarcity. This duty principally devolves upon the women, who, marshalled by a numerous body of Fetishwomen dressed in white, carry green branches in their hands, and go singing and dancing through the streets. During this ceremony, they call upon their gods to send them the

* Has this custom any connection with the Jewish ordinance for all the males to appear before the Lord?—*Vide* Deuteronomy xvi, 16.

blessings of " fish, corn, and peace ;" and the wild
clamour of their shrill voices is heard at a great
distance, as they continue shouting out, in a musical
chorus, this short prayer. At the same time, the
principal Fetishwomen throw heave-offerings of
corn bread, mixed with palm oil, upon all the
rocks and principal Fetishes. In seasons of drought,
too, they observe a somewhat similar practice ; but
if rain is long withheld, they go direct to the
Braffo Fetish in a grand procession, and seek the
intercession of the priests by offerings and sacrifices.

Great virtue is supposed to reside in one of the
principal Fetishes of Cape Coast, especially in the
matter of making the sea propitious for their fishing ; and upon the occasion of the death of an old
Fetishman who ministered at this altar, we remember having seen his body, which was tightly bound
up in palm-leaves, dragged by a long rope along
the beach and through the breakers, surrounded
and followed by a numerous crowd of howling
worshippers, who had implicit faith in the power
of the dead Fetishman to give them an abundance of fish.

They divide time into weeks, months, and the
seasons of the year. The division of the week into
even days, for which they have distinct names,

appears to have always prevailed among them, as well as the observance of one of those days as a sabbath of rest. The fishermen have set apart Tuesday for their day of rest, while the bushmen or agriculturists observe Friday. But in addition to this general ordinance, each individual is in the habit of paying great respect to the day of the week on which he was born. On it he dresses himself with more than ordinary care, abstains from all manner of business, and employs it in a more close observance of his Fetish. They have no means of computing a series of years, and can only reckon their age by a reference to collateral events. In the time of the African Committee, the regularity of the arrival of store-ships annually for the forts, afforded them the nearest approach to the enumeration of time; and during that period, it was customary to say that a person was so many store-ships old.

CHAPTER VIII.

Native marriages — Betrothals — Description of a young
virgin—African marriage cards—Causes of divorce —
Enslaving nature of the marriage contract—Curious
custom observed in reference to girls—Observances at
the naming of a child—African names—African lovers—
Curious case of disappointed affection—Murder of a wife
and children—The story of Adjuah Amissah—Circumcision—Customs for the dead—Expensive observances—
The cause of slavery—Laws respecting inheritance—
Day of annual remembrance —Extraordinary scene—
Human sacrifices in Ashantee and Dahomey—Custom
made for Governor Maclean.

It has been stated, that native contracts of
marriage are made by the payment of a certain
sum to the relations of the bride.* This sum

---

* In this we have another instance of resemblance between the customs of the African and the patriarchal age :—
" Ask me never so much dowry and gift, and I will give
according as ye say unto me ; but give me the damsel to
wife."—Genesis xxiv, 12.

varies according to the rank of the individual, from two ounces of gold (£8) to four ackies and a half (£1 2s. 6d.); but it is more frequently paid in goods than in gold. Betrothals often take place long before the female has arrived a marriageable age—sometimes even before she is born. Such being the case, it is needless to say that the inclinations of the lady are little consulted.

A desire to be connected with the family of a friend induces the African frequently to betroth mere children, which he does by presenting the parents with a flask or two of rum, and a piece of cloth. The acceptance of these destines their offspring to be the wife of the donor. There is, in consequence, great dissimilarity of ages; the child of fourteen being often united to the man of fifty. But the prevalence of polygamy makes this custom a hardship only on the part of the female, as the man has, in his youth and manhood, been already joined to several wives of more appropriate ages. This betrothal, however, is held perfectly binding on the family of the girl, who is henceforth regarded as the wife of the person betrothing her, and who narrowly watches her conduct, and frequently demands and receives compensation for the most innocent and unsuspecting liberties which she may allow other men to take with her.

Upon arrival at the age of marriage, which in this precocious country takes place about the thirteenth year, the girl is dressed out with most extraordinary care in rich silks, borrowed in many instances for the occasion. Her hair is completely covered with golden ornaments, consisting of doubloons, sovereigns, figures of serpents, fish, alligators, and crosses. Chains of gold hang down over her bosom, which is left uncovered, and her tawny skin is exquisitely painted in very delicate lines of white chalk, giving her the appearance of having on a tightly fitting vest of the finest lace. Armlets and anklets of gold encircle her wrists and feet, while the silk robe extending from the waist to the ankle is gracefully fitted over a neat bustle, and compressed by means of a broad silk girdle around her loins. There is often an appearance of great elegance in the naked simplicity of this attire, well suited to set off to advantage the trim little figures of the young virgins, whose delicate features, sparkling eyes, beautiful teeth, soft velvety skin, and fine rounded breasts, greatly add to the charm of their appearance.

There is, especially at this early age, an air of grace, of lively gaiety and effeminate softness, about the young African girl, which gives to her movements great beauty and gracefulness, and fills the mind with such agreeable impressions as we experience when contemplating a fine picture, a beautiful horse, or the airy and natural elegance of the young fawn. We see in her every glance, and in the unpremeditated ease of her motions, the buoyant elasticity of youth and health, revelling in the glad joyousness of mere animal existence.

As soon as she has been properly attired, she is paraded through the streets, attended by a numerous escort of her own sex, one of whom holds an umbrella over her head, to protect her from the sun, or rather, perhaps, to aid the effect of her elaborate toilet. They attract the notice of the inhabitants by singing a loud pæan in honour of her virginity, giving the bachelors to understand that she has arrived at the marriageable age. Soon after this event, if she has been previously betrothed, she is led home to her husband; or, if not betrothed, the publicity thus given to her charms soon attracts to her suitors for her hand. Previous to the consummation of the marriage ceremony, rum, tobacco, and pipes are given by the husband to the bride's family, which are distributed among the more immediate friends and relations, as proofs of their honourable alliance, a species of "marriage cards" in fact, to notify the event. In addition to this, a more general notification is sometimes given by a long procession of people, sent to the husband's house with presents of bread, yams, plantains, oil, fruits, and sheep, which they carry through the streets on their heads at the same time that they sing a song in honour of the event. These preliminaries having been gone through, the bride is led to the house of the new husband, who gives a feast to his friends upon the occasion.

It might be supposed that enough had now been done to acquaint the world they live in with all that it was necessary to know of the married couple. But "the spirit of jealousy," which in the African takes the form of a strong instinct, requires an evidence of the lady's purity. In the event of the husband being satisfied on this important point, he is obliged, as the Africans emphatically express it, "to give her chalk"—that is to say, he sprinkles her over the head, neck, shoulders, and breast with a thick powdering of white chalk, and sends her through the streets, accompanied by a train of singing damsels, who proclaim the praises and the honour of the young bride. But if he brings a palaver to the family—that is, if he accuse them of having passed off upon him a girl not a virgin, then he is entitled, if his accusation be found correct, to a restitution of the money expended in dowry to his wife, as well as the ordinary expenses attending the marriage, and, moreover, he can at once repudiate her. If there be truth in the accusation, the girl's family often persuade him to patch up the matter and hide her shame ; but if it be groundless, he is called before the elders, by the girl's father, who is required to produce " the tokens of her virginity."* This being done to the satisfaction of the judges, the husband is bound to pay damages for defamation, and the girl may if she pleases repudiate him without being obliged to make restitution of the dowry.

The desire for offspring is particularly strong among the African women, barrenness being considered a great reproach. It is the cause of much discord between husband and wife, and frequently leads to separations. Among the higher classes, a slave girl is generally given by the bride's family, to attend upon her in her husband's house. This slave, in many instances, becomes the concubine of the husband ; and her mistress, when she has no

* The practice, in cases of this nature, corresponds exactly with the Mosaical law.— *Vide* Deuteronomy xxii, 13—22.

children of her own, regards the offspring of her maid as her own progeny.*

Among the poorer classes the man and the woman sometimes live together, without any dowry having been paid, or only a single bottle of rum for the friends to drink upon the occasion. In such cases, the husband generally resides with the family of his wife, and gives his services to eke out the means of their common subsistence. Owing to the little community of interest between husband and wife, to which we have already adverted in our general view of the construction of society, and which leads them to consider themselves individually as members of distinct families, separations are of frequent occurrence, and easily made; the wife, under such circumstances, invariably returning with her children to her mother's family.

The causes of this separation are various. If the husband neglect his wife for a length of time to bestow his favours upon a rival, or grossly maltreats her, she may leave him without making restitution of her dowry;† but if she has become

* Of this we have also instances in the Scriptures, Sarai and Hagar, Leah and Zilpah, Rachel and Bilhah, Hannah and Peninnah.

† Exodus xxi, 10, 11.

tired of the connection, and wishes to leave him without cause, she is compelled to repay him the original dowry paid for her, with all other expenses and presents, which he may have made ; and if she has children, she has to pay him four ackies and a half (22s. 6d.) for every child which she has bore to him, as a reward for his proper fulfilment of the connubial duties. This latter part of the arrangement is often compromised, by the mother allowing her sons to remain with their father ; but in this case he has no pecuniary claim upon them, and cannot sell or pawn them.

Sometimes, not being able to make restitution of the expenses made by her husband on her account, she leaves her children in pawn to him for the amount; and they are obliged to serve him, until this sum, with 50 per cent of interest, has been made good. From causes like this, children have often become pawns and slaves in their father's house for life, and have descended as such to those who have succeeded him in the family inheritance. Connubial infidelity is punished by fine or damages awarded to the husband, which vary according to the rank of the individual from £1 to £10 ; and where polygamy prevails to such an extent, such a crime is of frequent occurrence. Indeed, many husbands make a trade of the frailty of their wives, and encourage them in their infidelity. But if the wife and the adulterer should prefer to live together, the latter may obtain her as his wife, by the payment of the husband's expenses on her account, without any additional compensation for the injury.

This arrangement, however, still leaves the wife liable to her new husband for this sum; and she cannot separate from him without making restitution. Even the death of the wife does not release her family from the debt of the dowry, which has either to be repaid to the husband, or another wife substituted by them in her place, upon whom the same debt in like manner devolves. And as her family are not released by her death; so neither is she at liberty to return to them upon the death of her husband. Unless she can pay to his successor the debt of dowry, she is compelled to become his wife also. The brother thus frequently becomes the husband of a brother's wife, or a nephew of his uncle's, according to the order of succession. A decent interval, however, is allowed to elapse before this second marriage is consummated, and sometimes the successor does not not seem inclined to marry her at all; but if another should have intercourse with her in the meantime, damages are exacted as if she had been really married.*

It is thus seen, that the wife in this part of Africa is regarded by the husband in the light of a pawn or pledge for the repayment of the money given to her family as dowry; and when we consider with what great facility the husband can add to the amount of the original debt, by other expenses incurred either by his wife or children, we readily perceive the very enslaving nature of the marriage contract. We have been thus particular in describing the laws regulating marriage, as it will afford the reader an opportunity of seeing how deep are the foundations of African slavery, since they are consequent upon the very propagation of the race.

A curious custom, originating in the superstitious belief of the people, prevails among them, in reference to a girl after conception. As soon as it becomes generally apparent that she is with child, her friends and neighbours set upon her, and drive her to the sea, pelting her with mud,

* By a reference to the thirty-eighth chapter of Genesis, the reader has a good illustration of this practice; and even in the meeting of Judah with his daughter-in-law, Tamar, he has before him an account of circumstance which might occur any day upon the coast of Africa.

and covering her with dust. During this operation they abuse her vehemently; and conclude the ceremony by tumbling her over among the waves. She returns unmolested to her house; and the Fetishwoman binds charms of strings and parrot's feathers about her wrists, ankles, and neck, muttering a dark spell all the while, to keep away bad luck and evil spirits. Without passing through this ordeal, they believe that her childbirth would be unfortunate.

It is considered very disgraceful to utter any cry of impatience during the pains of labour. The African mother must endure the pangs of nature with a stoical indifference, if she would not incur the taunts and reproaches of her neighbours. Upon those occasions, they make use of stools, such as were employed by the Hebrew and Egyptian women of old, and are generally surrounded by a crowd of visitors.

After childbirth, the mother remains unclean for seven days; and continues " in the blood of her purification," for even a longer period than was prescribed by the Levitical law. After the first seven days, during which she can touch nothing without rendering it unclean, she is permitted to attend to ordinary affairs within doors, but she cannot go from home, or take part in any ceremony, until the period of her purification be completed.   She then makes her sacrifice and offerings to her Fetish, is afterwards dressed out with extraordinary care, with a profusion of golden ornaments and rich cloths, and pays visits to her friends.   On these occasions, she is accompanied by a band of singing women, who sing a song of thankfulness for her safe delivery.   In these songs they express their gratitude, not only to the Fetish, but to all the inhabitants, considering that she is indebted in part to them for her recovery; for, inasmuch as no ill-luck had befallen her, it is evident that no one had wished her harm or bewitched her, or given her up to the vengeance of their Fetishes.   The very cordial manner in which they are in the habit of expressing their thanks to the individuals upon whom they make calls, perfectly conveys the impression, that they really believe themselves under the greatest obligations for their good-will and forbearance, of which they have sufficient proofs in the mere absence of misfortune.

Eight days after birth the child receives its name from its father, who proceeds with some friends to the house of the mother, if she does not reside in the same house with himself, which rarely is the case at such a time, as she almost invariably returns to her mother's house at this critical juncture. The father and his friends seat themselves in a circle at the gate of the house. The child is then brought out, and handed to him. After a short address and blessing, he bestows a name upon it, calling it generally after some deceased relation, or some particular friend still living, who assists at the ceremony, which consists in squirting a little rum from his mouth into the child's face. Libations are then poured out to the Fetish to propitiate his favour for the child, and the christening concludes with a jubilee among the friends. In addition to this name, however, the child takes another from the moment of its birth, derived from the day of the week on which it was born. These are for:

	MALES.	FEMALES.
Sunday	Quashie	Accoossuah.
Monday	Cudjoe	Adjuah.
Tuesday	Quabino	Abnebah.
Wednesday	Quacoe	Eccooah.
Thursday	Quow	Abbah.
Friday	Cofee	Effooah.
Saturday	Quamino	Ambah.

Until the child has arrived at an age to be of some use to its father in carrying on his occupation, whatever it may be, he gives himself very little anxiety about its training. He may occasionally be seen nursing it, and amusing himself with its prattle, beguiling an indolent hour in this manner; but more frequently he leaves it entirely to its mother's care.

It is thus brought up, principally, in the society of women and grown-up people, who place no restraint upon their conversation on account of its presence; but, on the contrary, speak and act as if their words and actions could have no effect upon its mind, and were not understood. It thus becomes familiar with thoughts, feelings, passions, and actions with astonishing precocity, and frequently startles us as often by its disgusting language, indicative of the foul pictures of life become familiar to its mind, as by its old-fashioned conceits of worldly wisdom. If the parents be engaged in agricultural pursuits, in which the man and the woman alike take a part, they are always accompanied to their plantations by their child, who has a small hoe placed in its hand to assist in the labour, at an age when its services can be of little moment. In like manner, even before it can handle any implement, it is carried about everywhere on its mother's back, seated upon a large bustle, and strapped round her by her upper garment. Thus roughly cradled, it is inured to all weathers and every kind of hardship, being carried about by the mother, whether she be engaged in carrying water from the pond, firewood from the forest, corn or vegetables to the market—in grinding her corn, or in hawking her petty merchandize through the streets.

This rude nursing is, generally speaking, so severe, that a very large per centage of children die in infancy. Those who escape this fate, undergo a variety of diseases incident to their mode of nurture, and until the ages of five or six years, their health seldom appears confirmed. A woman has seldom more than six or seven children, although we have known instances of as many as a dozen; but the average does not, at all events, exceed five, and of these, perhaps, no more than two or three arrive at maturity.

If the father be a fisherman, his child is to be seen at sea with him in his frail canoe, and handling a paddle, which he has as yet scarcely the strength to lift. Indeed, no sooner are the senses of the child awakened to the realities of life, than it becomes initiated into all the practical concerns which occupy the very limited attention of the parents; and as these are confined to the necessities, habits, and customs of a very simple and primitive mode of life, its education is readily and almost intuitively acquired.

Marriage takes place at an early age. The enjoyments of the African being chiefly of an animal nature, he delivers himself up to the gratification of his passions, unrestrained by any considerations except those of an irresolute prudence, which forms but a frail safeguard for virtue. Their frequent dances and merry-makings in the streets on moonlight nights, their often-recurring seasons of Fetish festivities, and their nightly serenadings, in all of which the males and females indiscriminately take a part, afford opportunities of forming *liaisons* which often disconcert the best-laid matrimonial schemes. There is indeed a freemasonry among the young, which begets a mutual understanding, which laughs at bolts and bars and all manner of restrictions, and compresses, into a few stolen moments, the sorrowful tale of kindred hearts.

It has sometimes been remarked, that the Africans are insensible to the tender passion, or that with them it merely amounts to instinctive indulgence. We by no means agree with this view of the case. Their love may, it is true, be unaccompanied by the romance, and sentiment, and refinement, which form the great charm of European attachments and of poetical description; but it is frequently distinguished by an order and a constancy full of distracting fears and doubts, and seeks its gratification, regardless of the greatest sacrifices. The African rushes into battle, shouting the name of his lady-love to inspire him to deeds of daring; the canoeman gives additional vigour to the stroke of his paddle at the mention of her name; the weary hammock-bearer plucks up a new spirit through the same all-powerful spell, and the solitary wayfarer beguiles the tediousness of his journey by a song in her praise. While seated round our watch-fires at Appollonia, we have frequently listened with a pleased attention to the fond pictures of home and love, on which their imaginations were wont to dwell, calling up ideas of increased fondness and attachment on the part of sweethearts and wives, from the dangers which they had encountered, the prevailing sentiment in the minds of the speakers being that of the swarthy Moor,

> " She loved me for the dangers I had pass'd,
> And I loved her, that she did pity them."

The obstacles thrown in the way of the union of lovers, occasionally lead to very disastrous consequences. We will mention an instance of this

kind which occurred some years ago. An attachment sprung up between two young people,
residing in the village of Aissam, in the Fantee
country. The girl was a pawn of her lover's
father, who could not be persuaded to allow them
to marry. He could not prevent them, however,
from cherishing a mutual passion in secret, which
they were not sufficiently prudent to conceal from
public notice. Reports of their too great intimacy
reached his ears, and he determined to put an end
to the annoyance by espousing the girl himself.
His son earnestly remonstrated with him upon
the cruelty of his conduct, declared the violence
and sincerity of his passion, which it was impossible for him to overcome, and predicted the
misery which must attend such an union.

The poor girl entreated him with tears and
prayers ; but he remained obdurate, and made use
of the power of a master to bend them to his will.
This ill-omened marriage was at length consummated ; but the spirit of jealousy which took possession of the husband, made it the fruitful source
of misery to him. Every look and action of the
wife were misconstrued. It was gall and worm-
wood to him to see her speak to his son, and the
loving glances of mutual intelligence, which they
knew not how to hide, were requited with great

harshness and cruelty. It did not appear that any improper intercourse had taken place between the lovers ; but the jealous fears of the husband would not allow him to believe them innocent. He persecuted his wife with great bitterness, and at last stripped her of her garments, and turned her out into the streets to be the laugh and scoff of her neighbours.

This treatment was more than she could bear. She went to her lover, reproached him as being the cause of her great misery, and besought him, swearing a great oath by the chiefs of the country, by Sir Charles M'Carthy and by the Fetish, to put an end to her sorrows and her misery, by shooting her, and afterwards killing himself. Highly exasperated, at seeing the state to which the object of his affections was reduced, and giving way in an evil moment, to the influence of the passions which had so long been consuming him, he rushed into his house, seized his musket, and shot the wretched girl through the heart. He then took a knife and cut his own throat ; but the wound not being mortal, he was brought to the hospital at Cape Coast, where he recovered only to be tried for the murder, and afterwards to be hanged—a fate, perhaps, scarcely merited, when we consider the aggravated nature of the feelings under which he committed the rash act. It ended the miseries of a life for ever clouded by the gloomy horrors of an unfortunate attachment.

Another victim of the laws, which regulate the system of human pawns, was guilty of a shocking murder, the result also of outraged affection. Having incurred a debt, he undertook to place his wife and child in pawn to his creditor, provided he was not able to pay it by a certain day. As the time approached, and he saw no means of satisfying the demands upon him, without the fulfilment of his cruel agreement, he shrank from the thought of giving over into the custody of another, those who were naturally so dear to him. Under the influence of the harrowed feelings, to which this idea gave rise, he stabbed his wife and child, and then laid violent hands upon himself.

The fame of Adjuah Amissah, a native of Cape Coast, is still kept fresh in the memory of the natives, by the songs which they sing in honour of her death. People are still alive, who remember the great beauty which hurried her to an early grave. She became the object of a devouring passion on the part of a young man of Cape Coast. Her relations, considering that her charms authorized them to expect a better alliance, refused to admit his addresses. This rejection so preyed upon the mind of the disappointed lover, that his life became insupportable, and he determined to sacrifice himself to his passion. He resolved, however, that Adjuah Amissah's family should dearly rue having spurned his suit, and in the spirit of an inextinguishable vengeance he shot himself, attributing his death to his unrequited love, and invoking his family to retaliate it upon his murderess.

It is the principle of the Fantee law, to visit the cause of such a calamity with a similar retribution, and when a person puts himself to death, " upon the head of another," as they express it—that is, attributes the cause of his act to another's conduct —that other is required to undergo a like fate. The family of the unhappy girl endeavoured to avert this fate by offering to pay a large sum in gold ; but nothing but her death would satisfy the vengeance of the youth's relations, and they appealed to the native authorities to vindicate their laws. All the mercy which could be extended to Adjuah Amissah, was to allow her a few days to lament with her friends her untimely end, and to have a silver bullet put into the musket with which she was compelled to deprive herself of life. She employed the few days of respite, in singing with her young friends her farewell dirge, and completed the cruel sacrifice by shooting herself.

These instances will show, that the love of the African is more than a mere animal instinct. Both men and women are at the greatest pains to render themselves mutually agreeable to each other. With this view, they decorate themselves with much care, and indulge freely in the greatest coquetry. They frequently exchange love tokens, and watch over the objects of their affection with a jealous eye. Contentions about a lover are of frequent occurrence, and lead to much strife and litigation. Amours are often carried on secretly, without the knowledge of relatives; but if a man betrays a virgin, he is compelled to marry her or to pay the price of her dowry, if the parents will not consent to the marriage.*

Women are considered unclean at particular periods, and are not allowed to touch anything in the house, or to approach their husbands. If they should accidentally transgress this law, they are subjected to heavy penalties. In some parts of the

* Exodus xxii, 16, "And if a man entice a maid that is not betrothed, he shall surely endow her to be his wife." 17, "If her father utterly refuse to give her unto him, he shall pay money according to the dowry of virgins."

country, and especially at Dixcove, they are not allowed to come into the house, or even to the town ; small huts being erected for them in the bush, where they remain until the period of purification.

Circumcision is practised among the natives of Accra. This rite is performed about the age of twelve or thirteen, the time observed by the descendants of Ishmael. They can give no other account of the origin of this practice, than that it had always been the custom of their ancestors.

The ceremonies observed upon occasions of death occupy a large portion of their attention. In view of this event, the head of a family summons around his death-bed his relations. He instructs them about the state of his affairs, and how his property was acquired, and how to be disposed of. He is most particular to furnish them with proofs respecting the acquisition of his pawns and slaves, mentions the names of the witnesses to the transactions, the circumstances under which they took place, and the sums paid for them, in order that his successor may be enabled to defend his rights, in the event of their attempting to obtain their liberty or redemption at the death of their master. He also recounts the names of his debtors, with the sums which they owe to him, as well as the debts which he owes to others.* His death-bed declarations, made in the presence of responsible witnesses, are always received as evidence in the event of litigation afterwards. Having made these arrangements, he calmly resigns himself to death, apparently unconcerned about a future state.

No sooner has the breath left the body than a loud wailing lamentation is heard proceeding from the house. The women rush into the streets with disordered dress and dishevelled hair, and utter wild sobbings and bursts of grief. There is something peculiarly heart-rending in the mournful accents of their voices. We have seen a mother suddenly bereaved of her child perfectly frantic with despair, violently beating her breast, and uttering such sharp agonizing screams, as the most acute bodily suffering could alone seem fit to elicit. The sting of a serpent, or the application of some horrible instrument of torture,

* The manner in which Jacob on his death-bed instructs his sons respecting the nature of their right to the cave in the field of Machpelah, which Abraham bought with the field of Ephron the Hittite, from the children of Heth, is an excellent illustration of the custom upon the Gold Coast. —*Vide* Genesis xlix, 28, 32.

could not produce more excruciating distortions than we behold them suffering, while writhing under the first stroke of their bereavement. Nature cannot long endure this vehemence of grief, and gradually they subside into a low monotonous dirge, broken by painful fits of sobbing and fresh bursts of uncontrollable anguish. Sometimes they lie low on the ground, unconsciously paddling with their fingers in the dust, and moistening it with their tears, without any interruption to their low monotonous wail.

Again they wander through the streets, regardless of every person about them, and entirely absorbed in their grief, which they vent in a loud, sorrowful, and sometimes defiant tone, as if they dared any one to gainsay their right to be perfectly miserable. The African seems to understand well the hopelessness of administering consolation, until the first paroxysm of grief be past. They pity and respect the mourner, but never obtrude a word of sympathy or comfort until the first natural impulse of the heart has had time to assuage itself.

The repose of night is often startled by the mourners thus going about the street; and while those on whom the affliction presses most heavily are delivering themselves up to the unrestrained expression of their sorrow, other relations are washing the corpse, and preparing it for the funeral obsequies. It is dressed out with great care in the richest robes of the deceased, and adorned with a variety of golden ornaments and beads. Thus apparelled, it is then propped up in a chair or sofa, and is ready to receive the visits of those who come to do the honours of its burial. Spirits and food are placed upon a table before it, and a close observation is necessary to satisfy one that life is extinct, so closely do the arrangements resemble the ordinary occasions of show and festivity, which he was wont to observe in his lifetime.

Relations, friends, and neighbours crowd to the house of mourning, and consider it necessary on their near approach to join in the universal wail. They speak to and address the dead, sometimes in accents of reproach for leaving them; at others, beseeching his spirit to watch over and protect them from evil. It is chiefly women who fill the chamber of death. The men generally seat themselves outside, and until the funeral custom is commenced, take no very active part in the proceedings; but the females, whether relatives or not, are very loud in their lamentations, and apparently deeply affected by the event. They appear to have at ready command an abundant supply of tears, which stream down their cheeks without intermission while they continue in the house, but which give place to smiles and laughter and the greatest unconcern as soon as they have turned their backs upon the scene.

It is customary for friends and acquaintances to bring presents to the relations of the deceased, to assist them in performing the funeral ceremonies in a becoming manner. These presents consist of gold, rum, cloths, and powder; and the more wealthy add fowls, a sheep, or a goat, and sometimes a bullock. Each succeeding party, as it arrives, commences a rapid discharge of musketry, accompanied by the beating of drums and dancing; and having expended their ammunition, they take up their station in the yard of the house, or in some convenient place near it selected for the purpose, and join in the songs, the dances, and general festivity which mark the occasion. These saturnalia often last for days and weeks, and are attended with scenes of great drunkenness and confusion. They represent that they are intended to distract the minds of the mourners, and to deaden the impression of grief; but we often hear, in the midst of all this noise, the wailing accents of the real mourner, who, seated in some obscure corner of the house, pours forth a continuous dirge, descriptive of the heavy loss sustained, of the good qualities of the deceased, and of the helplessness of those left behind, deprived of his protection.

There is often much beauty and simplicity of feeling expressed in these unpremeditated songs. A grave is dug in the floor of one of the rooms of the house ; and here the body, laid in a coffin, with rich cloths, gold trinkets and aggery beads, with rum and tobacco, and sometimes a considerable amount of valuables, is finally deposited. Sacrifices of sheep and bullocks, and fowls, are made over the grave. The more immediate relatives of the deceased are in the habit of shaving all the hair from their heads and persons, and of performing a long and painful fast. It is sometimes with difficulty that they can be induced to have recourse to food again at all. They are rendered unclean by the touch of a dead body, and may be seen going in procession to the sea, as soon as the grave has been closed, to sprinkle themselves with water, which is their process of purification.

Widows generally keep the house for many weeks after the death of their husbands, and maintain a constant watch over the grave. During this time, they neglect their persons, and partake most

sparingly of food.   On the day after the custom is
at end, the relations of the deceased, dressed out in
mourning cloths of dark blue baft, go round the
streets, singing a song of thanks to the people for
their assistance at the funeral, and calling for a few
moments at the houses of more intimate acquaintances, to thank them more particularly.   It is
considered unfortunate if a man approach a widow
before she has performed certain Fetish ceremonies
and sacrifices, which are supposed to have the
power of removing the ill-luck, and which seldom
take place until many months after the death of
the husband.   Whoever transgresses in this point,
is doomed to misfortune.   He is sure, they think,
to die in battle, to be drowned at sea, or to mis-
carry in whatever he takes in hand.

All these troublesome and ceremonious observances attending the obsequies of the dead, occupy
a very large portion of the time of the people, and
in seasons of great sickness and death they appear
to an observer to have little else to occupy their
attention.   They are also a fruitful source of debt
and slavery.   Let the consequences be what they
will, it is deemed a point of honour to make a
great show at their funeral customs, and they vie
with each other in performing these expensive
burials.   Even the poorest will pawn and enslave

themselves to obtain the means of burying a relation decently, according to the ideas of the country. The expense falls upon the heir of the deceased, who is often obliged to raise the funds by pawning some of his relations, which the laws of the country allow him to do, as head and master of the family.

Considerable sums are received in presents at the time of the funeral, but these are often consumed at the festivity. At all events, they are seldom a source of gain, as it is expected that the receiver will make similar presents to the donor upon the occasion of death in his family. The African has a strong desire to lay his bones among those of his own kindred, and dead bodies are frequently brought from long distances to be buried in the family house. On the approach also of a mortal illness, many strive to reach their homes to die among their friends. In many of the towns of Fantee, when a stranger or passing traveller dies among them, the inhabitants seldom bury him. The body is placed upon a wooden platform outside the town, with any property which he may have, to be claimed by his relations. If these be known to the natives of the town in which he dies, they are sent to and informed of the circumstance; but if they be not known, the body is allowed to wither and consume in the open air.

This custom does not take its rise from any superstition, or from want of respect to the dead; but from fear of the consequences attending his interment. The Fantee laws render the person who defrays the burial of the deceased responsible for his debts, and it is the dread of incurring this responsibility which leads to the barbarity of the exposure of the corpse. The operation of this law often brings heavy liabilities upon surviving relatives, in addition to the mere funeral expenses, as in many instances the defunct leaves little or no property behind him to meet the debts which may be brought against him, and which his nearest of kin is bound to pay. To avoid this liability, where the debts of the deceased are great, and his property nothing, the relations carry a small present to the authorities of the town, and deliver the body to them for interment. This forms a legal discharge from his debts; but it is not frequently had recourse to, as great disgrace is attached to any family who thus declines to bury their dead, and they prefer to incur debt, and even slavery to this reproach. The customs for the dead are not confined to the period of his decease. If his heir be wealthy, they are renewed at stated intervals and with increasing pomp.

At a certain period of each year, about the season of eating new yams, a general remembrance of the dead is observed throughout the land. We have been startled at a very early hour of the day set apart for this purpose, by the wailings and lamentations proceeding from every house. They commence the day by devoting a short portion of it to mourning for those who have died during the year, and their grief appears as loud and natural as on the first day of their loss. Members of a family come from a great distance to join in this observance. After they have sufficiently testified their sorrow by their cries and tears, the whole of the members of each family unite together, and proceed to their place of sepulture. They seat themselves around the grave, some on stools, others on the ground. They then address the spirits of the deceased, praying of them to accept their offerings, to guard the family from misfortune, and to bless and prosper them.

Old people record the good qualities of some ancestor, and urge the young to adopt him as a pattern for their conduct. They then pour out a libation of rum upon the grave, and strew it with corn-bread mixed with oil. After this they give themselves up to a day of festivity, dressing themselves in their finest clothes, and receiving and returning calls. Upon such an occasion the towns upon the coast present a scene of great excitement. The chiefs come out in their greatest state, and are carried through the streets in their basket palanquins, attended by crowds of very gaudily-attired retainers, who sing and dance, and beat their tom-toms. Old and young alike join in the general gaiety. They form themselves into small bands for the most part related to each other, and pass slowly round the streets, singing songs and dancing. They intermit this occupation to visit the houses of their friends, where they are generally regaled with spirits.

The great variety of costume, their showy colours, the rich dresses of the chiefs, their silverheaded canes, the large gold handles of their swords, their picturesque umbrellas, the lithe figures and sparkling glances of the delighted dancers, the rampant joy of the little children astonished at their finery, the contrast of their dark skins with the rainbow colours of their dresses, the wild cadence of their songs, the warlike sound of their horns, their noisy but stirring drums, and the confused hubbub of bewildered joy which seems to pervade the whole, form altogether such a combination as cannot be witnessed without a strange astonishment. The European residents who do not choose to close their doors against them are expected to receive their visits on this occasion. No sooner has one party been admitted, than others arrive in quick succession. They enter the house, often singing the praises of the person whom they come to visit, and whom they approach with a bold confidence, in curious contrast with the distant and almost fearful respect which they are wont to observe on other occasions. One sentiment of universal gladness appears to level all distinctions, and to place all ranks for one day upon a footing of happy equality. They eagerly press forward to shake hands, are profuse in their expressions of regard, of thankfulness to God and the Fetish for preserving the white man to see another year, offer prayers for his continued health and happiness, for an increase to his riches, and the blessings of peace in his time ; and having performed a dance in honour of him, they retire in the same merry spirit to give place to new visitors. During such extraordinary scenes of a total abandonment of a whole people, to what may be called a religious joy, incumbent on all by the rules of their Fetish worship, it is not perhaps to be wondered at, that the day does not close without indications of a very general inebriety. . It is rare, however, to hear of any quarrels during their excesses upon this occasion ; good-will everywhere prevails, and the hearts of all appear so steeped in the overflowing of an exuberant joy, as to be incapable of harbouring an unkind or an ungenerous thought of another. This avoidance of strifes and contentions is so different to their conduct on ordinary occasions of festivity, that we cannot help attributing it to a sense of the religious nature of this festival.

In the account which we have given of their funeral customs, we have not adverted to the practice of human sacrifices, as it is no longer followed, throughout the whole of the extensive districts at present enjoying British protection. In Ashantee, Dahomey, and until lately, in Appollonia, a frightful sacrifice of human life often takes place upon these occasions. The authorities at our forts get their first intimation of the death of men of rank in Ashantee, from runaway slaves, who have made their escape from these terrible immolations, and who do not consider themselves safe until they have placed themselves under the protection of our flag.

Upon the death of a king, scarcely any one is safe, as his relations and executioners rush into the streets and slay every one they meet. Their only protection is to remain within their houses, which are not violated to gratify this bloodthirsty impulse. In Fantee, the people are now satisfied to content themselves with the sacrifice of sheep and bullocks, and they make up for the diminished consequence of their sacrifices, by the noise and extravagance of their loud discharges of musketry. The practice of firing guns at burials must have arisen from an attempt to imitate the custom of Europeans at their military funerals. It is now, however, perfectly incorporated with their own ideas of befitting respect for the dead. The quantity of powder expended on these occasions is sometimes enormous; and nothing can exceed the noisy confusion of such a scene.

Upon the occasion of the death of Mr. Maclean in 1847, the town of Cape Coast, for the long period of fourteen days, presented the appearance of a continued cannonade. All kind of business was suspended. Day by day new parties arrived from distant parts of the country, who, taking up a position in front of the castle gate, continued for hours their loud discharges of musketry; and even months after, upon the arrival of any chief from the interior, who had not visited Cape Coast since his death, he considered it necessary before attending to any other business, to pay this last mark of respect to his old governor.

CHAPTER IX.

Modifications introduced into the native laws and customs by the English magistrates—Certificates of emancipation—Alterations in the law of marriage—Difficulties attending the question of slavery—Mode of proceeding in reference to runaway slaves—Recruiting—Commotion excited by the enlistment of slaves—Major Hill's prudent conduct—A slave's idea of emancipation—Practice pursued in reference to Ashantee runaways—The King's regard for oaths—Condition of the slave—His instinctive obedience—Causes of severity—The Donko—His inferiority to the Fantee—Extent of the internal slave trade—System of pawning—Summary of the African character—Resemblance between the state of society on the Gold Coast and the accounts given in the Scriptures of the nations of antiquity.

From the account given of the customs and the social condition of the people in the two preceding chapters, in which we have described them in their natural state, without adverting to the great modifications which European influence is now rapidly effecting, the reader will have little difficulty in perceiving the very enslaving nature of their institutions. He will also understand how hopeless must be their sudden emancipation, seeing that slavery is no abnormal development, but a natural and spontaneous growth. Many circumstances in their condition, both externally and internally, have tended to aggravate its nature, and multiply its forms. Among these, the export slave trade deserves a pre-eminent notoriety, as it fostered, if it did not originate, that spirit of lawless acquisition which placed the weak entirely at the mercy of the strong, who knew no mercy. But its total suppression along that line of coast, and the ameliorating influence of a more humane administration of justice, and of a consequent increased and increasing consideration for the rights of individuals, have checked its violent lawlessness, and modified its natural severity, as well as extinguished many of the sources of slavery, and opened a way for the redemption of all who can be roused to seek their freedom by their own industrious exertions.

Scarcely a day passes that the English magistrates are not called upon to examine into the validity of a master's right to the persons held in slavery by him. These cases are brought into court by a summons issued at the instance of the slave. An investigation is made into the nature of the master's right, which is often found to be invalid ; in which case the slave is unconditionally emancipated. But if the master's title to him be valid, according to the laws of the country—that is, if he can prove that a money value was paid for himself or his ancestors—then the slave is obliged to pay a redemption price for his freedom. The ordinary amount paid in such cases is two ounces of gold (£8).

Certificates of freedom are given under the hand of the magistrate, which are treasured up with a jealous care, to be produced in after times, when any attempt is made by the master or his heir to resume his alleged right, which they sometimes do upon the death or absence from the coast of the magistrate before whom the case was decided. These certificates have an additional value in their estimation, as they are considered to place the individuals holding them under the more immediate guardianship of the government, which effectually protects them from imposition and oppression. The writer has, during a long period of magisterial duties, had occasion to grant some thousands of these, and has found them to be, with rare exceptions, a very efficient safeguard. It may be that the redemption price has not been in all cases paid by the person redeemed, and that he is not entirely relieved from a state of servitude. His relations often advance the money, which lays him under obligations to them, which he can only requite by his services; or a new master may have been induced, upon promise of his obedience, to do the same good office for him. But as his emancipation from slavery has been effected, his new obligations merely amount to a common debt.

English interference is also putting an end to the enslavement going on through the laws regulating marriage, by disallowing the repayment of the dowry, and the expenses incurred during cohabitation, in all cases except where the wife leaves the husband without just cause. The protection also given against accusations of witchcraft, the extortions of the Fetishmen, the rapacity and injustice of the native tribunals, and an exorbitant usury, is fast closing up the avenues of very fruitful sources of slavery. The effect of missionary teaching is also exercising a beneficial influence in restraining the customs for the dead; while the spirit of improvement, which education and commercial enterprize have evoked, is directing numbers to the means of independence.

At the present time, the Gold Coast essentially exhibits all the symptoms of progress in every phase of its existence. There is a vitality of change diffusing its innumerable currents throughout every

class of society, and giving expansion and force to
an entirely new class of ideas, affecting the moral,
religious, social, and domestic condition of the people.
A taste for many of the European necessaries and
luxuries of life, and a partial assimilation in the
construction of their houses, in dress, in manners,
and in religion, are becoming daily more observable ;
and even where little external change is perceptible,
there is nevertheless going on an extensive modi-
fication of ideas, feelings, and customs, paving the
way for a more general conformity to the usages of
civilized life.

This infusion of new ideas and desires has effected
a very marked improvement in the habits of the
people, serving as an invigorating principle of action,
and substituting activity for idleness, and habits of
useful industry for idle mummeries and barbarous
amusements. If no interruption be given to the
gradual advancement thus hopefully commenced,
their social elevation will be rapid and continuous,
but we must carefully guard against any rash inno-
vations, and trust their development more to the
influence of the progress of opinion, than to compulsory enactments. On more than one occasion,
our influence has been greatly endangered by a
threatened interference with the state of slavery
existing among them. This is the question about

which we have to apprehend the greatest difficulties. Our colonial authorities in Downing Street appear to shrink from the very mention of the word slave by one of their governors, and have scarcely ever been induced to look the difficulty fairly in the face. The consequence has been that a species of timid disavowed policy has been pursued by our Gold Coast governors in reference to this subject. Our settlements appear to be regarded, as far as this question is concerned, as entirely British territory, and subject to British law, without ever taking into account that the British authorities are exercising a most beneficial influence over at least a million of natives occupying a most extensive range of country. Our governors are instructed not to deliver runaway slaves, who are supposed to recover their liberty as soon as they reach a British fort, and no slaves are supposed to exist within our jurisdiction.

No one, who has read the account which has been given of the state of slavery in the country, can believe in the possibility of a sudden emancipation without the total disruption of society and universal anarchy. If the governor is to countenance the slave in renouncing his obedience to his master, by harbouring him, where is he to find an asylum for him, or how support him? for it is only within the walls of our forts that we could shield him from his master ; and if this asylum were opened for all the discontented slaves in the country, it would be an utter impossibility to find room to contain them, or to provide means for their subsistence. In consequence of the great squeamishness upon this point, our governors have been obliged to grapple with the difficulty as they best could, without entering into any details in their communications to the Colonial Office.

The plan hitherto adopted has been to examine into the slave's complaint against his master, and if the treatment which he has received should appear to have been very bad, he receives a certificate of his liberty, and public opinion assents to this decision, as only a proper check upon the severity of a cruel master. But if, as is more generally the case, his complaint be frivolous, he is restored to his master, who gives security for his kind treatment of him. Were certificates of emancipation given to every slave who chose to run away, the natives generally would throw off their allegiance, cut off all intercourse with our settlements, and punish the disobedience of slaves in a very summary way— by putting them to death. Slaves are the only property of many people in the country, and no reasoning can convince them that the forcible taking of them away is not as much a theft and a robbery, as if they were deprived of their value in gold. In consequence of this state of slavery, the present governor, Major Hill, has had many difficulties to encounter in raising a local corps of three hundred men. It was only from the class of slaves that he could expect to get his recruits. Many of these came to the castle for enlistment, and the governor, in pursuance of his instructions, refused to deliver them up to their masters.

A great commotion was excited in the country by this proceeding, which was on the point of bringing the governor into hostile collision with the people. The chiefs promised to produce the requisite number of men, provided the governor would stop his enlistment, and they seemed prepared to run all hazards to defend their rights. Major Hill acted with great prudence upon the occasion, and prevented an insurrection, to which the forcible defiant execution of his instructions must inevitably have led. But he was obliged to wink at an arrangement made between the recruit and his late master, by which the latter was to receive monthly a portion of the pay until the sum of £8, the price of his redemption, should be made good. If such a feeling was excited about the enlistment of a few recruits, whom they acknowledged to be necessary for the purposes of

government, and employed for their own protection, it is not difficult to imagine the effect of a
sweeping measure of emancipation, or even the
non-recognition of their right to hold slaves. It
was not so much against the individual loss that
they contended. Even those who were not injured
by the enlistment were as loud in their complaints
as those who sustained this loss. They were contending for a principle which affected the whole
frame-work of society, and which nothing short of
an irresistible compulsion could have induced them
to renounce. Nor, admitting the possibility of
upholding the slaves in a renunciation of their servitude, should we, in their present primitive state,
consider it conducive either to their moral or social
advancement.

The control of a master is necessary to restrain men within the limits of order essential to
the preservation of society, until their faculties
and pursuits have been sufficiently developed to
enable them to feel their self-interest to consist in
honest industry, and in the observance of the laws
which regulate the community of which they form
a part.

Most of the crimes at present committed on the
Gold Coast are perpetrated by vagabonds, who
have absconded from their masters, and who live

by theft and plunder; and the only excuse or extenuation which the criminals themselves give for their conduct is, that they had no person to look after them, and support them.

When Dr. Madden explained to a number of slaves at Accra, that the English government did not recognise slavery, and that they were free, they asked him to provide for their subsistence; for unless the queen intended to give them something to eat, they would prefer to serve their master who supplied their wants.

Another difficulty which our Gold Coast government has to contend against, is the disposal of runaway slaves from Ashantee. It was stipulated in our treaties with the king, that his fugitive, subjects should be re-delivered to him in the same way that Fantees, flying into his dominions, were to be restored to the governor. This arrangement was necessary to prevent malefactors escaping punishment. But in many cases, the runaway Ashantee seeks a refuge from the fate which is likely to overtake him at the murderous customs which are often taking place at Coomassie, and a natural repugnance is, of course, felt about surrendering him.

Our position and power, however, do not enable us to follow the course most consistent with our feelings. If we were to refuse to deliver these runaways, the King of Ashantee would retaliate by seizing all the Fantees in his country, where a large number may at all times be found prosecuting their trade. He has also the means of cutting off all intercourse with his country, a measure which he invariably adopts upon occasions of misunderstanding with the governor. If redress were refused, war would be the consequence, a calamity in the present hopeful state of progress which would go far to undo the good which has been already effected, and which of all things is most anxiously to be avoided. Under these circumstances, the governor is obliged to mediate as he best can, and refuses to deliver up the runaway, except upon condition of sufficient security being given that his life will be spared.

Although this restriction must be galling to the king, yet he is induced to submit to it, rather than incur the risk of a doubtful war, into which he and his chiefs would not hesitate to plunge if such a vital question as the non-surrender of runaway slaves were involved in the issue. The security given for their safety is simply " the king's great oath," taken on his behalf by his messengers. There is no instance known of this oath given under such circumstances being violated. We remember a case, which will show the fearful regard which the king has for oaths.

Upon application being made for some runaways, the messengers were required to take the usual oath before they were surrendered. The refugees, however, were not satisfied with this oath alone, and positively refused to return to Ashantee, unless the king's messengers would give additional security for their safety, by "kissing the white man's book." They did not hesitate to agree to this, as they were perfectly satisfied that the king's oath would not be violated, and that, therefore, there could be no danger in kissing the book. But when they returned to Coomassie, and the king found that they had bound him, not only by his own, but also by the white man's oath, he became alarmed, lest any accidental injury might happen to the persons thus protected, which might bring him under the penalty of its violation; and to get rid of the liability, he sent the refugees back to the Fantee country, preferring to lose them to the risk of incurring an unknown danger.

It will be thus seen, that both to avoid insurrection among the Fantees, and the horrors of a war with Ashantee, the British authorities are compelled to adopt a policy with regard to this slave question, which appears never to have been openly avowed, and which is never brought under the notice of the Colonial Office without exciting a feeling of uneasiness, and calling forth a renewed declaration that slavery cannot be recognized within our settlements upon the Gold Coast, thus throwing back upon the governor the responsibility of its recognition.

We have considered it fair to place this question fully before the public, and to represent it in all its breadth and deformity; and we justify the policy pursued, as the only one adapted to the state of the country, and in every respect the most humane, and best calculated to promote the well-being and advancement of the people. We must look for the only legitimate extinction of slavery in such a state of society, to the gradual and extensive diffusion of wealth and Christian knowledge, through a series of successive generations. They are now fairly entered upon this career, and the only assistance we can give, is to protect it from interruption, and to multiply the means of its acceleration. Each succeeding year will render our progress less difficult, by providing us with an increasingly efficient ally, in the gradual education of the people. If it be offensive to English ears, to hear that a slave does enter our forts on the Gold Coast without acquiring the liberty which, by our laws, the very touch of our soil is held to communicate, then must we relinquish our establishments in this country. But if we do not choose to sacrifice to a proud boast, the power which circumstances have given us of conferring blessings of civilization on a benighted and enslaved race, let us boldly persevere in the course upon which we have entered, in a firm reliance that Providence will prosper our exertions in so righteous a cause.

The condition of the slaves in the countries under our protection is by no means one of unmitigated hardship. In ordinary cases, the slave is considered as a member of his master's family, and often succeeds to his property, in default of a natural heir. He eats with him from the same dish, and has an equal share in all his simple enjoyments. He intermarries with his children, and is allowed to acquire property of his own, over which, unless under very extraordinary circumstances, his master exercises no control. He sometimes even acquires wealth and consideration far superior to his master, who may occasionally be seen swelling his importance, by following in his train. They address each other as " my father " and " my son," and differ in little in their mutual relations from the respect and obedience implied in these endearing epithets.

We see in the whole of their domestic economy a complete transcript of the patriarchal age; the same participation in the cares, and sorrows, and enjoyments of life; the same community of feeling and of interest; and the same external equality, conjoined with a devoted obedience, so marked and decided, as to assume the form of a natural instinct. This quality in the mind of dependants has a tendency to destroy the idea of personal accountability. The will of the master is in most instances more than a counterpoise for the volition of the slave, who yields obedience to his commands with an instinctive submission, without the intervention of any external compulsion, and often under circumstances where the natural inclination of the slave is opposed to the particular conduct required of him. Slavery of body and mind is thus thoroughly engrained in the constitution of the African. We have known cases of murder having been committed at the command of a master, and against the remonstrances of the slave, who however does not refuse compliance; and we have seen how completely the will of the master has been considered the test of the slave's conscience, by the perfect unconcern of the latter respecting the deed, and the absence of any idea of his accountability for it.

Scarcely would the slave of an Ashantee chief obey the mandate of his king, without the special concurrence of his immediate master; and the slave of a slave will refuse obedience to his master's master, unless the order be conveyed to him through his own master. This perfect identification of the mind of the slave with that of his master has no doubt given rise to the master's accountability for the acts of his slave, and to the laws which affect them. He has to pay his debts, and to make compensation and restitution for every injury committed by him, either wilfully or accidentally. This responsibility may be a cause of the kind and considerate treatment so often observable, the master's interest being so closely involved in the conduct of his slave, as to render him anxious to attach him to his person, and to engage his affectionate obedience. It will also account for the isolated cases of harshness and cruelty which occasionally come under our observation, the vindictive slave having it in his power to cause his master much annoyance and expense, for which the latter can only retaliate by corporal suffering. Where this discordant spirit exists, the master, after repeated ineffectual attempts to reclaim an incorrigible slave, gets rid of the annoyance by selling him.

There does not appear any limit to the extent of punishment which a master is permitted to inflict upon his slave. He is considered so entirely his property, that he may with impunity put him to death; although from applications for freedom, on the ground of severe personal injury, such as the loss of an eye or a tooth, there is reason to believe that, during some period of their history, the slave was protected by a more humane code of laws.

We have heard a slave argue for his emancipation on the score of the accidental loss of an eye, in his master's service, from the recoil of a branch of a tree, and appeal to a traditionary law* which entitles him to this compensation.

Like the Hebrews, the Fantees make a distinction between the slaves, their countrymen, and those who have been taken in war, or purchased from another tribe. The latter, until they become amalgamated by a long period of servitude, and by intermarriage, do not receive the same considerate treatment. They are considered an inferior race, with the ordinary class of whom

* " And if a man smite the eye of his servant, or the eye of his maid, that it perish, he shall let him go free for his eye's sake."—Exodus xxi, 26.

it is thought derogatory for the daughters of the
land to intermarry. The burden of the labour of
the country falls upon them. Immense numbers
of these slaves are being annually imported into
the country, through Ashantee, from the countries
near the range of the Kong Mountains. Many
of them, on their first arrival, manifest an extraordinary degree of stolidity and brutishness, and
exhibit a very low type of intellect and breeding.
They pass under the general name of " Donko,"
a word signifying a slave in the language of the
interior, and which, from the great stupidity of
these creatures, has come to be a word of reproach,
tantamount to " fool." They are naturally a very
obstinate, perverse, and self-willed race, upon
whom it is difficult to make any impression by
kindness. It is very difficult also to coerce them
to labour; and yet, notwithstanding their many
bad qualities, the Fantees eagerly purchase them
from the Ashantees. They vary in price from
£6 to £8, girls and boys being sold at a considerable reduction. They have scars on the
face and person, distinctive of their native tribes;
some with semi-circular lines covering the whole
face, some with a few scarred lines on each cheek,
some with a single raised mark upon the forehead,
and others seamed and scarred over the whole

of the upper part of their persons. Among this servant race, we find also a good many mongrel Moors, little superior to the others.

If they arrive in the country at an early age, they are by no means slow in acquiring knowledge, and become very useful to their masters, and sometimes obtain a consideration equal to the native of the country, intermarrying with the Fantees, and becoming members of their families. But if the Donko be grown up before his arrival upon the coast, he generally remains a dull, stolid beast of burden all the days of his life. It is only by comparing the native Fantee with these, that we are sensible of the very great advancement of the former, who appears a very civilized being in comparison with this foreign race. And yet these are not altogether devoid of some of the better qualities of our nature. They evince much sympathy and compassion for each other, and readily assist one another in their difficulties. A common fate appears to unite them by the ties of a patriotic attachment, and they delight to sing, in the place of their captivity, the songs of their native land. Their treatment by their masters depends much upon their own conduct, for interest, as well as natural inclination, make the Fantee a kind master. The great stubbornness of the Donko, however, often brings down upon him a severe chastisement, to which he submits with a sullen insensibility. Some thousands of these are added to the population of the country under our protection every year. Various considerations have induced the local government to tolerate this internal slave trade, which it would be difficult to suppress. The objects of it are either taken in war by the Ashantees, received as tribute from subjugated states, or purchased by them. If they were not bought by the Fantees, many of them would be sacrificed at the Ashantee customs, or kept in a worse bondage in that country. By being brought into the countries under our protection, their lives are spared; they receive a more humane treatment; they are shielded from oppression, and are placed within the influence of a higher degree of civilization. Their condition, in every respect, is improved by the change, and the second generation becomes an effective addition to a by no means superabundant population.

It will be seen, then, that while the diffusion of wealth and the progress of knowledge are creating a spirit of industry, and exciting a desire for greater freedom among the native Fantees, a fresh tide of slavery is pouring into the country from another direction. It may be questioned how far this state of matters is to be approved. But when we reflect, that the Ashantee wars are not undertaken expressly to supply this demand; that the transfer of the slaves from the Ashantee to the Fantee country is not adding to the ranks of slavery generally; that it greatly ameliorates the condition of the slaves in question, and brings them and their descendants within the scope of many civilizing influences, to which they would otherwise have remained strangers; that, moreover, an increase to the population is desirable to bring out the resources of a rich and fertile country, we are warranted in concluding that the cause of general civilization and of humanity is advanced by this movement. It is not unreasonable to hope that, after centuries of progress, the tide of emigration may again recede into the interior, carrying with it the seeds of civilization and Christian knowledge.

Besides the native-born Fantee slaves, and those purchased from the interior, there remains to be noticed another species of slavery existing, under the name of "pawns," to which we have already adverted. It has been seen that individuals form, in the present state of commerce, no small portion of the currency of the country. To obtain a loan or pay a debt, a master does not hesitate to place one or more of his family, or slaves, in temporary bondage to another. The terms of this contract are, that the pawn shall serve his new master until such time as the person pawning him shall make good the sum lent, with 50 per cent. interest; the services of the pawn, even if they should extend over a great number of years, counting for nothing in the liquidation of the debt. If a woman has been pawned, her new master has the right to make her his concubine, and her children continue to serve him also.

The cruel operation of this system will be best illustrated by an example. We will suppose A. to pawn his daughter B. to his friend C. for the sum of two ounces. He finds it impossible to redeem her, perhaps, under a period of many years, during which time we will suppose her to have borne seven children to her master. A. now is anxious to redeem his daughter, but he cannot do so without paying C. the original amount with interest, and four ackies and a half (22s. 6d.) for each child, which raises the original debt of two ounces (£8) to four ounces fifteen ackies and a half, or £19 17s. 6d. The money paid on account of the children is regarded as an equivalent for their maintenance.

If A. has had to borrow the money to effect this redemption, which frequently happens, it will be seen that the original sum of two ounces would go on accumulating at a rate which must eventually leave this family in a state of hopeless bondage. The death of the pawn does not cancel the debt. A. must substitute another pawn in her place, or pay the amount; but in this case B. generally, though not invariably, foregoes the interest. Neither is the master of a pawn, like the master of a slave, responsible for his pawn's debts. These recoil upon the head of the person pawning her.

A father cannot pawn his child without the concurrence of the mother's relations, unless she also be his slave. Neither can a mother pawn her child without the father's consent; but if he cannot advance the sum required, then she can do so. We have always regarded this system of pawning as much worse than actual slavery, and we have seen but too many of its victims irrecoverably reduced to perpetual bondage. The English authorities have greatly mitigated its hardships, by refusing to consider the loan in any other light than that of a common debt.

After the account which has been given, the reader will now be able to have a clear comprehension of the nature and condition of slavery upon the Gold Coast. It would appear that it is greatly influenced by the state of social progress, and that its exactions become more rigid in proportion to the advancement of a people. The closer the points of resemblance between the master and the slave, the easier will be the yoke; and where the improvement of both go on simultaneously, all distinctions gradually become effaced. We see the gradual operation of this process among the Fantee masters and their native-born slaves, while the diffusion of greater wealth among the former, and of increased knowledge, renders the condition of the " donkos," an inferior class, more truly that of a degrading servitude, and widens the distance between them and their masters.

We have now taken a view of this interesting people under a great variety of aspects, and would fain hope that we have provided the reader with data to enable him to form a correct estimate of their condition. Before closing this subject, we are anxious to compress into one brief sketch a general picture of their every-day life; but we shrink with conscious inability from the attempt, for who can portray all the varied shades of existence which so distinctively characterize them in their idiosyncrasy of temperament, in their domestic and social relations, in their superstitious observances, and in their acts as members of the body politic? What daring hand shall arrest the ever-changing expression of this Protean race? What daguerreotype shall fix its various lineaments? What strange and sudden contrasts of feeling, what unaccountable alternations of purpose, what eccentricities of conduct, arrest and puzzle our observation! Joy and sorrow, reckless gaiety and gloomy despondency, exaggerated hopes and distracting fears, unbridled passion and humble meekness, ardent love and cool indifference, fierce hate and cordial friendship, prodigal profusion and griping avarice, atheistical unconcern and bigoted superstition, sway by turns their versatile minds, and with a rapidity of change which startles and confounds us. In whatever relation of life we view the Gold Coast native, we equally behold him the creature of some momentary impulse, which he seeks not to conceal, and knows not how to repress.

Born beneath the rays of a tropical sun, with a clear and serene sky over his head, seldom ruffled by lowering storms, his character partakes largely of the gaiety of external nature, and his exuberant spirits are in unison with her bountiful profusion. Freely as the earth ministers to his wants, supplying him with the necessaries of life almost without the penalty of labour, as thoughtlessly and unstint-

ingly does he make use of her bounties. Fond
of his ease, and loving to indulge a quiet, volup-
tuous indolence of disposition, he can seldom be
roused to much bodily exertion, unless enticed by
the prospect of obtaining the means of festivity,
to which he delivers himself up with the most
determined abandonment. Possessed of high
physical qualities, and patient in the prosecution
of his object, when once his mind is fairly bent
upon it, he is capable of enduring the severest
toil and the greatest privations; but unless his
affections are engaged in his work, he soon relapses
into inactivity and indifference, and leaves his task
unfinished. Such does he appear in his purely
native condition; but brought into contact with
Europeans, and rendered familiar with a system of
thought and of action, differing in so many respects
from his own natural heedlessness of disposition,
he soon learns to conceal his emotions, and to
disguise his real sentiments, and ends in becoming
an accomplished hypocrite. He is by no means
deficient in intellectual faculties; but they are
cramped and paralysed by the strong superstitious
bent of his mind, and we see on many important
occasions his whole reasoning powers thrown
prostrate by this prejudicial agency, in the very
moment of their triumphant vindication.

His views of external nature, of his own condition, and of all the circumstances which affect it, are, in consequence, narrow and limited, and confined within the spell-bound circle of his prejudices, which nothing but the clearest comprehension of his interest is able to break. His memory is strong and retentive, and he dwells with a garrulous minuteness upon the recollections of his youth. His lively imagination delights to feed itself with pleasing reveries; but it is gross, sensual, and unrefined. He is naturally eloquent, speaks with an easy and fluent grace, with suitable and appropriate action, and clothes his ideas with a simple and natural imagery. He has frequent recourse to parables, and dark and enigmatical sayings, which he never deigns to explain, taking an apparent delight in leaving the minds of his hearers to puzzle out his hidden meaning. He is fond of repartee, dearly loves a joke, the coarser the better, and has a most lively sense of the ridiculous. He delights in rude and barbarous merriment, and in noisy and turbulent carousals. He is quick and irascible in his temper, but easily appeased if the injury be unintentional or slight; but when deeply offended, it is impossible to regain his favour without a peace-offering, in the shape of a present of rum, or a sheep, with which he makes a libation or a sacrifice to his Fetish " to give him a good heart."

In the excitement of the moment, he is sometimes perfectly blinded by his passion, and commits acts which he deeply repents, and which he would undo the very next instant. With all this, he is, in ordinary intercourse, particularly observant of the courtesies of life, is slow to give offence, often dignified in his deportment, regardful of another's consequence, and tenacious of his own. Indignity and slight rankle deeply in his heart, and are seldom forgiven. His affections are keen, but not durable, and the impressions of sorrow are soon effaced. His joys and his sorrows equally find vent in spontaneous song, and at morn, noon, and night the streets re-echo with the loud catch of the bacchanal, the impassioned lays of the lover, and the plaintive notes of the mourner. He is slow to form friendships, but firm to retain them, and will often sacrifice his money and his comfort to help a friend in distress. He does not easily give his confidence to an European, although he may treat him with the greatest outward deference and respect. He is quick in discovering peculiarities of temper and conduct, and treasures up words and acts, to enable him to form a true estimate of character. Once satisfied of the white man's truth, honour, and justice, of his favourable inclinations to black men generally, and of his sensible and judicious views, nothing can exceed the childlike obedience with which he gives himself up to his guidance.

It is not upon a short acquaintance that this influence is established; but when it has been confirmed by time, and an uniform consistency of conduct, the European is in a position to break down the strong barrier of his prejudices. He is, in short, a truly natural man, in all his corruptions, and in many of his virtues, and formed like ourselves for such slow and gradual development of his moral and intellectual faculties as the constitution of our common nature will only admit.

Upon a general contemplation of their whole customs and manners, as well as of the construction of their minds, we cannot help being forcibly struck with their great resemblance, in many respects, to the state of society handed down to us, in the earliest records of the human race. Everything in their ideas, in the idiom of their language, in their worship, and in the naked simplicity of their manners, betrays their primitive condition, and

convinces the attentive observer, that he is contemplating a race of men, who, though old in
their generations, have, in most of their essential
characteristics, an unmistakable impression of an
early stage of society. We seem to be transported
back to the patriarchal age, and to be living among
a people in the same state of simple nature. It
requires no effort of the imagination to bring
before the mind's eye the manner in which the
characters recorded in Scripture thought and
spoke and acted, as we have daily in our sight
living representations of human beings actuated
by similar impulses which find vent in similar
modes of expression and action.

The extraordinary coincidences in many particulars of the manners and customs of the Africans,
with those of the Hebrews and other Eastern nations, must lead us to the conclusion that we see
in Africa a transcript of these, corrupted by the
uncertain light of tradition; or that the human
mind, in certain stages of its progress, and under
the influence of similar predisposing causes, exhibits
an uniformity of bias and development so truly
astonishing, as to be argument sufficient to set at
rest the cavils of philosophers respecting original
inferiority of race.

The observation of such a state of society clearly demonstrates the necessity of the Mosaical dispensation, to wean the human race from the gross idolatry into which it had fallen; for it could only be by types and symbols that man, constituted as he is, could receive into his mind an idea of the attributes of the true God. It is impossible for him to arrive at the knowledge of a holy, just, and merciful God, without revelation; and this revelation could only be conveyed to him through the medium of the senses, aided by reflection, comparison, and abstraction. Man can form no idea of such a being, as there is nothing in the material world which would convey it to his mind. He can, therefore, only transfer to his idols his own imperfect attributes, and by worshipping them, the reaction of his own depravity would recoil upon himself. In this consists the corrupting nature of all idolatry. We deify the worst passions of our nature, become in consequence assimilated to the objects of our worship, and thus aggravate our natural depravity by a most besotting infatuation. To this cause must we attribute the stagnant nature of the Fantee mind, it being impossible for it to rise above the standard of its worship.

And now let us consider the necessity of types and symbols as the only means of conveying a revelation of a perfectly holy, just, and merciful God. In the infancy of language, there is no term by which an abstract idea can be conveyed. If the Christian missionary were confined to the use of the Fantee language, he could only throw into the minds of his disciples the idea of a perfectly holy God by a process of symbolical comparisons similar to those instituted among the Jews. We have seen in the Mosaical account given us in the Scriptures, that this idea was conveyed to the minds of the Jews by separating the animals into clean and unclean, the first step in the comparison of purity. The beasts selected for sacrifice were to be from the clean class, and not only so, but from those of that class without spot or blemish, thus conveying another degree of purity. These sacrifices were to be offered by the priests, a class purified, and set apart for the office. Before they could be offered, both the beasts to be sacrificed and the priests had to be washed and purified; and even the sacrifice could only be made in the court of the Holy of Holies.* Thus, by a series of comparisons, God's holiness was contrasted with the highest degree of earthly purity, as neither the people, the priest, nor

* The writer is chiefly indebted to a work entitled "The Philosophy of the Plan of Salvation," for a confirmation of the views which he had himself formed upon the subject.

the sacrifice were considered sufficiently pure to come before him, and the idea of his perfect purity was thus established in their minds and engrafted upon their language. They were led to see by the same system of types, that God's perfect holiness became the standard of his conscience in the punishment of sin by death, thus revealing his justice, while the vicarious substitute of the sacrifice for the sinner impressed them with an idea of his mercy.* If the missionary had not the power of transferring these ideas from his own language into that of the Fantee, it would be impossible to originate them in the mind of the latter without the teaching by similar types. As it is, the poverty of the language makes it a most difficult process of instruction; for it is impossible to disjoin the abstract idea formed by outward objects, and represented by a word derived from them, from the object which originated it. From this cause, we have never been able to listen to the performance of Divine service in the Fantee tongue, without being shocked by the irreverent ideas constantly

---

* We have not been able to discover that there is in the African's mind any idea of the substitution of the sacrifice for himself, when he sheds the blood of men or beasts in sacrifice. He merely yields to a traditionary practice, which he does not understand.

obtruded upon the mind by the use of vulgar words applied to sacred emotions, which we have felt assured the generality of the hearers understood in their literal acceptation. Even with the assistance of circumlocution and illustration, they find it difficult to express the full force of abstract ideas, and the native interpreters are constantly having recourse to the substitution of the English words which represent them. This is a difficulty which can be overcome by time alone, and the adoption of words of foreign extraction into their language. At present, shades of meaning can only imperfectly be expressed by degrees of comparison, and the Fantee language must be much enriched before it can become an efficient medium of Christian instruction. We thus see the slow and progressive steps by which new ideas are originally impressed upon the mind, and can by reflection upon this tedious process, which is necessary according to man's constitution, more easily make allowances for the misapprehension of pagan converts to Christianity upon many points of faith and doctrine.

CHAPTER X.

No written language—Difficulty of reducing the Fantee
to grammatical rules—Proficiency of young scholars—
Prevalence of written communications in the English
language—Music—Musical instruments—Workmanship
in gold — Tanning and dressing leather — Weaving—
Dyeing — Agriculture — Native process of grinding—
Palm wine—Manufacture of oil—Introduction of cotton-
growing—Mr. Freeman's model plantation — Exports
—Imports—Dress—Houses—Taste for European luxuries—Hospitality.

ALTHOUGH it will be perceived from the delinea-
tions which we have given of the Gold Coast
natives, that considerable regularity exists in
their forms of government, in their laws, in their
worship, and in their social relations, and that they
have the appearance of having attained to this
degree of advancement long before their intercourse with Europeans ; yet viewing them as a
whole, we cannot consider them as having advanced
beyond the state which Europeans would denomi-

nate barbarous. There is among them no trace of a written language, no hieroglyph, nor symbol, nor anything corresponding to the painted stories of Mexico or the knotted *quipos* of Peru. Their communications are altogether oral, and their history is a blank. Nor have Europeans been successful in reducing their language to grammatical rules, which would be necessary to its being written in the Roman character.

Educated natives have frequently failed in making communications in writing, in their native language, intelligible to each other, from their disagreement about the sounds of words, and the consequent employment of different letters to represent them. We do not even know, that it is desirable that much anxiety should be felt to remedy this defect, for the sooner their own language gives place to the English, which is rapidly spreading among them, the better will it be for their progress in knowledge and civilization. It will be as easy for the African to acquire a knowledge of the English language, and to write it, as it would be for him to acquire the grammar of his own, and to reduce it to writing. Teachers find little difficulty in instructing them to read and to write English; and the African boys, who are sent to school at an early age, would bear a comparison of their proficiency with English children of the same standing. Their powers of imitation are very strong. They acquire with ease the art of penmanship, and seem capable of changing their style of writing at will, according to the copies set before them. A native clerk will, in the course of a week, be able to copy his master's hand so exactly, as to puzzle him to discover whether it is his own or his clerk's.

There are nearly a thousand of these children receiving instruction at the schools of the Wesleyan Missionary Society, who are yearly sending out from them some hundreds of young people, very tolerably educated. The uninstructed natives make use of these to keep their accounts, and to communicate by letter with each other ; and they are now so widely scattered over the country, that every village, even in the remote interior, has one or more of these scribes residing in it, who supplies the inhabitants with the means of communicating with their friends at a distance. Letters are received daily by the governor and magistrates from Ashantee, Akim, Wassaw, Assin, Appollonia, and all the towns of Fantee. Many of the chiefs have a secretary in constant attendance upon them, very frequently their own sons, who have received their education at the schools. The merchants also receive written orders for goods, from trading correspondents in the interior. In short, the people now generally have all the advantages which are to be derived from the written communication of their wants and feelings.

Parties to a suit in our courts are particularly anxious to avail themselves of this method of representing their cases to the magistrates. They think, and think rightly, that it is a check upon the infidelity of the interpreters. Representations of their cases are therefore carefully drawn out, and handed in upon the court days. Many of these communications are of a very extraordinary nature, from the simplicity of their details, and the plain unvarnished statements of their complaints. Some of the scribes charge a high price for their services, varying according as they estimate their importance. The ordinary sum given for writing a letter is about ten-pence, but we have known an instance of four pounds having been paid ; and when the scribe was afterwards brought up for his exorbitant charge, the only excuse which he thought it necessary to give for such extortion was, that he " considered it necessary to teach these ignorant people the value of literature."

With such ready means of communication, the greatest facility is afforded in carrying on the trade of the country, as well as in furthering the views of the government. Let the reader contrast this state of matters, and the general peace and security which it implies, with the distracted state of the country twenty-five years ago, and he can scarcely help being astonished at the rapidity of the progress made.

Africans are passionately fond of music, and have an excellent ear for it. The native airs are very simple, consisting merely of detached bars. Their songs are chiefly a species of recitative or chaunt, with a short chorus. They are often improvised, the principal performer giving out a line, and a band of choristers joining in the refrain. He stands up while the others are seated around him, and turns from one to another, while he pours forth his unpremeditated lay. As one gets wearied, or his invention fails him, another takes his place, and continues the amusement, which frequently lasts for hours. They are very expert in adapting the subjects of these songs to current events, and indulge in mocking ridicule, in biting sarcasm, in fulsome flattery, or in just praise of men and things, according as circumstances seem to demand. The bravery of a chief, the beauty of a young girl, the liberality of a friend, the avarice of a miser, the poltroonery of a coward, the affection of a mother, and the disappointments of a lover, form indiscriminately the themes of these extemporaneous effusions.

If a white man were to pass these songsters, while thus employed, they would quickly seize upon some peculiarity of his character, whether good or bad, and celebrate it aloud, amidst the unrestrained merriment of the by-standers. Even a passing stranger whom they had never seen before, would come in for a share of their notice, and some eccentricity of look, of gait, or of apparel be quickly fastened upon as worthy of praise, or of ridicule. This habit of publishing the praise or shame of individuals in spontaneous song, exercises no little influence upon conduct ; for the African is most sensitive to public opinion, and dreads being held up to ridicule, while the incense of flattery incites him to actions which will gain for him the admiration of his countrymen. In this way these singing men and women become the organs of public opinion, and supply the place of our journals and gazettes. The acrimony of their censure is sometimes so severe, that it leads to contentions, especially when a whole company or division of a town forms the subject of a derisive attack.

Their musical instruments are neither numerous nor of great compass. They have a drum formed of the trunk of a tree scooped out, and a skin stretched over one of the ends. The larger kind is carried on the head of a bearer, the drummer following behind and plying his sticks. The smaller drums are hung round the neck, and beaten either with small sticks or the fingers. These drums or tom-toms are in very frequent request. No merry-making can take place without them. They appear to have the same stirring effect upon the Fantee, which the bagpipe has upon the Highlander. He dances franticly at their sound, and even amidst his most rapid evolutions keeps time with astonishing accuracy.

It is laughable to observe the effect of this rude music upon all classes, old and young, men, women and children. However employed, whether passing quietly through the street, carrying water from the pond, or assisting in some grave procession, no sooner do they hear the rapid beats of a distant drum, than they begin to caper and dance spontaneously. The bricklayer will throw down his trowel for a minute, the carpenter leave his bench, the corn-grinder her milling-stone, and the porter his load to keep time to the inspiriting sound. Even the cooper rivets his cask and drives his hoops, keeping time to some native air, and the inhabitants, in default of other music, may be seen dancing to his strokes.

They have also a species of guitar, called a sancho. It consists of a square hollow box with a neck attached to it, having eight strings in two rows, supported perpendicularly by a bridge. It is played with the fingers, and has a soft soothing effect. This instrument is chiefly employed to give expression to the more pensive moods of the mind. The lover and the mourner find consolation in its notes, which they accompany with their voices. It is principally in the moonlight nights that we catch the low sound of their plaintive melody.

They have also a long flute which discourses sweet music. Its notes have a most pleasing effect upon the ear, and are inexpressively sweet. It is impossible to listen to it without desiring to hear more than the musicians bring from it, their airs being only broken fragments of melody, and not a finished composition. They play this instrument generally in bands of five or six, and pretend to be able to converse together upon it.

Their most martial instrument is the horn, which is made of an elephant's small tusk. It has simply a hole perforated in the side near the small end and requires good strength of lungs to blow it. Every chief has a horn-blower and a special air of his own. It has a bold, loud, defiant sound, and rallies the retainers round their master. A chief never travels without a retinue of armed followers, his drummer, and horn-blower. He announces his arrival in a town by the martial note of his horn; and even before he is seen, the inhabitants can distinguish by the peculiar sound who it is. These notes always express some short sentence descriptive of the chief's prowess, or of his contempt for others. Great offence was given by an Anamaboe chief, by the meaning conveyed in his trumpet note. It appeared to the town's-people to say "Who are you?" in slighting allusion to them, in comparison with the horn-blower's master.

They have also gong-gongs, rattles, and casta-nets, which assist in adding to the noise, in which they take such great delight. Many of them have learned to play upon English fifes, flutes, flageolets, and bugles. They pick up our airs with the greatest facility, and play them tolerably after hearing them a few times.

The arts have not made much advance in this part of the world. They are ingenious workers in gold, and make rings, chains, and brooches, which would do no discredit to an European artist. They mould the gold in every variety of shape, of beasts, and birds, and creeping things, and adorn their persons with these ornaments. They know something of the tanning of leather; but the Fantees are inferior to many of their neighbours in the art of dressing it. They have attained to some proficiency in pottery. Their earthenware is good and serviceable for holding water and cooking. They also mould images from clay, and bake them. We have seen curious groups of these in some parts of the country. Upon the death of a great man, they make representations of him, sitting in state, with his wives and attendants seated around him.

Beneath a large tree in Adjumacon, we once saw one of these groups, which had a very natural appearance. The images were, some jet black, some tawny-red, and others of all shades of colours between black and red, according to the complexion of the originals, whom they were meant to represent. They were nearly as large as life, and the proportions between the men and women, and boys and girls, were well maintained. Even the soft and feminine expressions of the female countenance were clearly brought out. The cabboceer and his principal men were represented smoking their long pipes, and some boys upon their knees were covering the fire in the bowls, to give them a proper light. There is no apotheosis of the dead intended by these representations : they are simply monuments to their memory like the statues of our own great men. No care is paid to their preservation after they have been set out for exhibition, but there they remain until they crumble to pieces. It is chiefly women who are employed in making these figures.

They also weave, making use of a small loom upon the same principle as the English hand-loom. They spin the thread from the cotton which grows in the country ; but they more commonly make use of thread out of English cloths, which they pick to pieces. The web is seldom broader than four inches, and is interwoven with a great variety of colours. Many of their cloths are elaborately wrought, and are sold among themselves at high prices. The Appollonians make fine grass cloths, which are strong and durable. They make strings, nets and ropes from the fibres of the plantain and cocoa-nut-trees. They are acquainted with dyeing, and use red, blue, yellow, and a green formed of a mixture of the blue and yellow. Their blue dye especially is very good and durable. Blacksmiths, carpenters, masons, coopers, tailors, and shoemakers now ply their busy trades throughout the land.

Their agriculture is still in a very primitive state. They have neither plough nor beasts of burden to assist in the operations of the field. Their chief products are corn, yams, cassada, ground-nuts, plantains, and bananas. Besides these, they have a great variety of fruits, which appear to grow spontaneously without much attention to their cultivation, such as pine-apples, guavas, limes, lemons, oranges, papaws, custard-apples, sour-sops, a variety of apples, called the Cashew apple, the Cormantine apple, and the sweet apple, melons, pumpkins, ochros, a species of musk cherry, and many kinds of peppers.

They have also the cocoa-nut and the palm-nut, from which they compress the oil, which forms the staple of the export trade. They cultivate a species of gourd, which grows to a great size, and is very serviceable to them. They are used for bottles, calabashes to drink from, water-pots, and trays. They sometimes bring the palm oil to market in them, and we have seen some capable of containing eight gallons. The sugar-cane and cotton-tree also appear to have been long naturalized to the soil, if they be not indigenous. But in addition to the fruits and vegetables which appear indigenous to the country, many others can be raised with moderate attention.

Mr. Freeman has a model farm or plantation, about seven miles distant from Cape Coast, which is a perfect nursery of every description of vegetable production. Perhaps there is not anywhere to be found, within the same limited compass, such an extensive variety. Over and above all the native products, he has successfully cultivated grapes, figs, arrow-root, coffee, radishes, turnips, carrots, beet, cabbage, peas, potatoes, onions, beans, &c., &c. He has also a variety of trees, and plants, and flowers, among which the cinnamon-tree and the rose are conspicuous. He has given the name of Beulah to his beautiful plantation, which being situated in the neighbourhood of a small mission station, where there is a chapel and school, and in the midst of a rich district, presents a fine landscape to the eye, and the most agreeable impressions to the mind, as forming the nucleus of the regenerating influences which are to ameliorate the moral and physical waste of the people and their country.

The natives prepare the ground for the seed by cutting down the matted thickets with the bill-hook, and leaving the more valuable fruit-trees and plants in the midst of their fields. The heat of the sun soon renders the withered bushes fit to be consumed by fire, and the ashes are scattered as manure over the ground. They seldom extract the roots, and simply turn up the ground between them with a hoe, and deposit the seed. More care is taken with their yam and cassada plantations, which are carefully kept clear of weeds, and staked and trimmed. The pistache, or ground nut, is also grown in raised beds, which require considerable attention to keep clean. They do not seek to cultivate more than is necessary for their annual consumption, but if a demand is made upon them for corn for exportation, they are eager to raise it for sale, and have the means of giving a large supply. They live principally upon bread made from the Indian corn, and upon yams and plantains, which they mash, or cut up into pieces, making a vegetable soup, which is highly seasoned with peppers. The corn is prepared for bread, by being ground upon a large stone, slightly concave, by means of another smaller stone roller, with which they squeeze the grains. The larger stone is raised a few inches from the ground in a slanting position ; the women stand behind it, and stooping down, move their arms, and the upper part of the body backwards and forwards, as they keep rolling the smaller stone over the corn. A vessel is placed upon the ground to receive the meal as it falls from the stone. This work is always performed by the women, generally about daybreak, when "the sound of the grinders" is heard in all the streets. They mix the meal with water, leaven the dough with a bit of stale bread, roll it up in a plantain leaf, and bake it in their small earthen conical ovens.

They do not make use of much animal food, not that they do not care for it, but because it is not abundant. They have not many bullocks in the neighbourhood of Cape Coast, which is not favourable for their pasturage. There are pigs, sheep, goats, turkeys, fowls, and ducks; besides game, such as deer, bush-pig, buffaloes, hares, partridges, &c. ; but they are by no means numerous. Dried fish forms their chief relish for their vegetable diet. In addition to what they cure themselves, there is a very considerable supply imported by the Americans, which is eagerly purchased. They make a very pleasant and palatable wine from the palm species of trees. This is done by up-rooting the tree, lopping off its leaves, and perforating the trunk. They place a calabash at the puncture, and burn some dried twigs under the tree. The sap is thus forced to the orifice, and received into the pot, into which it distils for several days at the rate of about a gallon a day. A good tree will yield about twelve gallons.

The wine is fresh and very pleasant to drink when new; but if allowed to stand for some hours it ferments rapidly, and becomes pungent and intoxicating. The natives are very fond of this beverage, and drink great quantities of it, preferring it in its strength. Sometimes the tree is not cut down; but the extraction of its sap destroys its vitality. It is the same species of palm-tree that produces the nut from which the oil is made. The nuts are placed in a large mortar built of stones, and pounded with sharp-pointed stakes, to separate the external husk from the stone. The husks thus separated are then gathered up, put into an earthen pot with water, and boiled. The oil ascends to the top, is skimmed off, and collected into separate vessels. These nuts are so full of oil, that it spirts out upon a pressure of the hand. They also make another drink from the corn, which is not malted. It tastes somewhat like small beer, and is called pittau. This drink, also, by being allowed to ferment, acquires considerable intoxicating properties.

The soil of the country is rich and fertile, and yields most abundant returns. Property in it is acquired by bringing it under cultivation. All the land in the neighbourhood of a town is considered as belonging to the inhabitants generally ; and the man who first cuts down the bush, and grows a crop, is regarded as the proprietor of the portion thus occupied. There is so much unoccupied space, however, that until lately property of this kind was little regarded. And it is perhaps the best evidence of advancement that litigations about a disputed title to ground are now of very frequent occurrence. The progressive development of the resources of the country is forcing upon the natives the conviction, that cultivation is the best and most legitimate source of wealth. A strong impetus in this direction has been given by an association of gentlemen who are attempting to introduce the cultivation of cotton as an article of export, and several of the native chiefs and others begin to give their attention to it; while the people generally are only waiting the result of the experiment, to undertake it, if it shall be found to answer. We do not think that there is much doubt about the success of a cotton plantation, if properly attended to. The labour of a grown person can be obtained at two dollars per month without any additional expense of board or maintenance.

The exports of the Gold Coast are gold-dust, ivory, palm-oil, corn, ground-nuts, malagetta pepper, and gum copal. The three articles first enumerated, form the staple of their commodities. The principal supply of gold is received from the Ashantee traders. It is found generally in the soil of the country in small dust; but the beds of rivers yield the largest quantities. There are also mines, where it is obtained mixed with red loam and gravel, and pieces of white granite. Many slaves are employed in collecting it throughout the Ashantee country.

From the River Barra, and from the province of Gaman, the largest supplies are said to be obtained; but the policy of the Kings of Ashantee, in preventing intercourse with the interior, does not enable us to speak with much certainty upon this point. It is also got in abundance in some parts of the Akim country, which appears to be as prolific as Ashantee. There are mines in Wassaw and Denkera. The Dutch government took some trouble to work a mine in the former country, but from the bad selection of the spot, from the sickness of the miners, and the unfitness of their apparatus, it was attended with little success, and is now abandoned. In most parts of the Fantee country, there is a slight impregnation of the soil with it; but it hardly rewards their imperfect process of separating it. They take a calabash partly full of earth, mix it with water, and agitate it. The particles of gold sink to the bottom, and the earth is thrown away. By continued processes of this description it is entirely separated from the earth, and found in minute grains deposited in the bottom of the calabash. It is also found near Winnebah in lumps of granite, which are pounded and sifted in the same manner. There can be little doubt that it will yet be found in parts of the interior in large abundance and in rich veins. We have ourselves seen a lump of eleven ounces, and Dupuis speaks of having seen at Coomassie lumps of the weight of four pounds. It would not appear that the quantity of gold exported from the Gold Coast has increased of late years. On the contrary, if we are to consider the statements which have been made on this subject correct, it has greatly decreased. Mr. Swanzy, in his evidence given before a parliamentary committee, in 1816, gives it as his opinion that a hundred thousand ounces of gold were annually produced. This is nearly double the quantity at present exported.

We are also dependent on the Ashantees for our supplies of ivory. Our exports of this article are now very insignificant. It would seem that the elephants are far less numerous than they were, or that the interior market for ivory has been closed against the Ashantees. The manufacture of palm-oil has greatly increased, and is still increasing. It is entirely produced by the natives living under our protection, who bring it, sometimes on their heads, in pots of five and six gallons, a distance of forty miles. The operations of trade are greatly impeded, from the want of beasts of burden, or any navigable river, the time of the people being so much occupied in the mere carriage of their produce to market. The trade, however, is steadily increasing, and is capable of a much greater though gradual development. We do not despair in the course of some years of being able to add cotton to the number of the exports.

The imports are cotton goods, silks, velvets, woollen stuffs, spirits, wines, tobacco, iron, brass, copper, lead, hardware, earthenware, cutlery, guns, powder, flints, salt provisions, house furniture, beads, cowries, tea, sugar, beer, and an endless variety of the ordinary articles of consumption. The commercial spirit is very strong in the African. The whole population are traders to a certain extent. It is the delight of the African women to sit in the market-places under the trees, exposing their wares for sale, or to hawk them through the streets from door to door, and from village to village. Their trade, however, is as yet little more than a barter of one commodity for another.

The Gold Coast natives are particularly fond of dress. The simplicity of the national costume does not admit of any other variety than what can be obtained by change of colours and of texture. It consists of an under girdle called a shin, which is tied round the loins, passed between the thighs, and the ends secured to the folds at one side. They are particular in having this part of their dress of the finest texture. It is very frequently of silk, of a showy colour, and they allow the ends or fringes to fall down the side of the leg, that it may occasionally be seen upon any disarrangement of the upper robe, which is thrown round the left shoulder, passed under the right arm, and readjusted in graceful drapery from the left, covering the whole person, with the exception of the right shoulder, arm and breast, which are left exposed.

These robes are made of all kinds of Manchester goods, of silks, of velvets, and of their own

rich country cloths.   The patterns and colours are
selected according to the taste of the wearer, some
preferring a neat modest print, while others delight
in gaudy contrasts of colour.   Wealthy people
indulge in frequent changes of apparel, and have
an immense variety of these robes.   Even the
poorer classes have several changes, and always a
good handsome cloth to wear on gala days.
Sandals are worn by the better classes, which they
remove from their feet as a mark of respect.*
They leave them at the entrance of a room when
they pay a visit.   They also salute Europeans, and
sometimes each other, by slightly removing their
robe from their left shoulder with the right hand,
gracefully bowing at the same time.   When they
wish to be very respectful, they uncover their
shoulder altogether, and support the robe under
the arm, the whole of the person from the breast
upwards being left exposed.   While labouring,
they often remove the upper robe altogether, or they
gird it in a large ample fold round the loins.†

The females have an under girdle similar to that
worn by the men.   To this is attached, behind, a
large bustle of a conical shape, extending about a foot

* This would also appear to be a traditionary usage of
great antiquity.

† " Gird up now thy loins like a man."—*Job* xxxviii, 3.

from the person. A robe is passed round the body from the waist to the ankle, and tightly secured immediately above the bustle by a broad outer girdle. This is the whole attire of a young unmarried girl. The breasts, shoulders, arms, and neck, are left perfectly uncovered. Older females wear an additional cloth, which is passed round under the arms, and meets the lower robe or petticoat, leaving only the shoulders, arms, and neck exposed. They are equally anxious with the men to set off their persons to advantage, and occupy no little portion of their time about their toilet, of which the proper adjustment of the bustle is their chief study. The size of this extraordinary appendage varies according to the consequence of the wearer, always increasing in proportion to her dignity. Both sexes make use of beads and gold as ornaments for the neck, wrists, and ankles.

Notwithstanding the bare exposure of so much of their persons, it does not strike us as indelicate, the dark hue of their skins taking away entirely from the naked appearance, and serving as a covering. Their fine smooth skins are, indeed, their principal beauty, and they take care to preserve them carefully. Their habits are cleanly. They wash their whole persons once, if

not oftener, during the day, and rub their skins
over with a little pomatum and other unguents,
which are so thoroughly absorbed by the friction,
as not to leave any unpleasant greasy appearance.
This is found to be a very necessary preservative
against the hard, drying action of the sun.   Such
are the national costumes of the men and women ;
but, like everything else in their condition, they
are being largely encroached upon by a growing
taste for our European style of dress.

Their houses do not exhibit much architectural
decoration, or great variety in their accommoda-
tions ; but even the very poorest have ample
shelter in proportion to their simple necessities.
The lowest class of dwelling which we have observed is to be seen in the neighbourhood of the
Saccoom river, near Accra, and at some fishing
hamlets between Axim and Dixcove.   These consist of small conical huts, thatched over with grass,
huddled together like so many hay-cocks upon the
sand, and with only a small aperture, through
which the occupant makes his ingress and egress
upon his hands and knees.   The appearance of
these kennels betrays at once the poverty, the
filth, the ignorance, and lazy habits of life of those
degraded creatures, who live principally by gather-

ing shells for lime-burning. The next in degree to these are the small hamlets in the interior parts of the country, the houses of which are, for the most part, composed of walls of bamboo and other stakes, plastered over with mortar, and thatched with plantain and palm-leaves. These huts consist of one, two, or more apartments, and have square holes to serve the purpose of windows and door-ways, which are closed up at night, by a bamboo fence drawn over the apertures, and secured inside to keep out the beasts of prey.

Some of these huts, of higher pretensions, have window shutters and doors, with all the advantages of hinges and bolts. The smaller villages are entirely composed of huts of this description. They are generally in the neighbourhood of the principal farms and plantations, and have been erected for the convenience of the labourers, who very possibly have dwelling-houses of a better description in some of the principal towns of the district.

Until within the last twenty-five years, there was so little security in the country now enjoying British protection, that men dared not live in detached dwellings. The population of a district was compelled to congregate in large towns for mutual protection. Long tracts of forest or jungle,

without a vestige of a human habitation, inter-
vened between these towns, in the immediate
neighbourhood of which they were obliged to cultivate their small patches of ground, without ven-
turing to any distance from their homes. The
great tranquillity, however, which the country has
enjoyed since the close of the last Ashantee war,
and the effective system of control under which
the natives generally have been brought by the
government, have entirely obviated the necessity
for thus herding together. Detached huts and
small hamlets have been and are springing up on
every side, and now give to the country not only
the appearance, but the reality, of greater populous-
ness and more extensive cultivation. There is in
consequence at present going on a partial depopu-
lation of the larger and more central towns, which
do not afford sufficient scope for the spirit of
greater industry evoked by the security and protection now universally felt.

But while the most industrious members of
these communities are thus carrying their labour
into new fields, and planting themselves in various
directions, where, seated beneath their own palm-
trees, they are enabled to enjoy in peace and comfort the fruits of their industry, they nevertheless
maintain a close connection and constant inter-

course with the parent towns in which their family houses are situated, and where their ancestors are buried. As yet these are emphatically considered their " homes," while their new dwellings in the wilderness are merely regarded in the light of a temporary convenience. In consequence of this idea of the transient nature of these new residences, they have been erected without any view to great comfort and durability, and consist chiefly of wattles and thatch. There are, however, decided indications that ere long their connection with the parent town will become nominal.

This is seen in more substantial houses being substituted for these temporary hovels, and in the neglect and dilapidation of the family houses in the towns. Greater independence is enjoyed in their rural retreats, where the whole population consists of one or two families, connected by relationship, than where they form a component part of a large town, subject to local regulations, under the immediate eye of their chiefs or head men, and exposed to the constantly recurring " palavers," which constitute the employment of the Fantees, when living together in large numbers. Daily the intercourse between their old and their new houses becomes less frequent ; longer intervals elapse betwixt succeeding visits; chiefs and head men grumble at the desertion of the houses, and remonstrate with the owners. These promise to return and make faint excuses for prolonged absence; but captivated with the happy independence and easy abundance of a country life, they gradually come to limit their visits to stated occasions of public festivity or annual custom-making. At last the disjunction is completed by the fallen roof and broken-down walls of the old family house, always to be, but never repaired.

The Fantee country, at the present time, bears in the general aspect of its towns and hamlets, the traces of this progressive change. The principal towns are deformed by heaps of roofless walls in all stages of decay, while substantial houses of higher pretensions are being built upon new sites in uninhabited parts of the country.

These houses are built of mud, or "swish," as it is called when prepared for use, which is done by mixing the earth with water, and tramping it with the feet. It is then collected into a heap, covered over with straw, and allowed to ferment for some days. Having thus acquired great adhesive qualities, it is built in successive layers of about eighteen inches high at a time. The hot rays of the sun perform the operation of baking it as effectually as an oven, and give to it the tenacity, consistence, and hardness of a brick. Their ordinary plan of construction is in the form of a square, the rooms forming its sides, and enclosing a quadrangular space, of dimensions proportionate to the size of the side rooms. The entrance is through a door or gateway, leading into one of these rooms, which is generally kept as an open lodge, through which to pass into the inner square, and in which the chief or head man is in the habit of keeping his drums. On the side of the square, fronting this lodge, the floor of the apartments is raised about a couple of feet from the ground, and is altogether open towards the square, or yard. Sometimes there is only a part of it open; a small space at each end being set apart for rooms. The other two sides of the square consist of rooms with doors and windows, their floors being on a level with the ground; or, as in the meaner class, of raised and open sheds, as already described.

These houses have rarely any windows opening to the outside, so that the entrance through the gateway is the only means of external communication. The greatest privacy is therefore enjoyed by every family, even in the centre of a town, as they can attend to the household affairs in the open air, within the square, or under the open sheds or rooms forming its sides, without being seen by their neighbours.

Of course there is some variety in the arrangements of the different houses, according to the taste of individuals ; but the prevailing, and what may be termed the purely native style, is such as we have here described. In houses of recent erection, the open apartments are now giving place to rooms with doors and windows, there being seldom more than one open apartment in the square. They frequently consist of a succession of these quadrilateral buildings and yards, the number being in proportion to the consequence and riches of the individual, and the size of his family. A small door of communication at one of the corners leads out of one square into another. The females of the house occupy one of these interior sets of apartments, where they perform the domestic duties of the establishment—grinding corn, pounding foofoo, cooking and preparing food. The fireplace is in the centre of the yard, and consists of three small clay cones placed close together in the form of a triangle; the cooking utensils rest between these, and the wood of the fire is on the ground beneath them; the smoke rises into the open air, and as the yard is closed in by the walls of the house, and there is not frequently much wind, the atmosphere is often thick and smoky during the operation of cooking.

There is frequently a second story upon one side of the square, and sometimes upon all. This is considered necessary to meet the idea of a white man's house, which they think it so desirable to imitate.

We have observed that the walls of these houses are built of mud, or swish. They are substantially roofed with stout sticks and thatch, which for the most part overlap the walls some two or three feet, and afford an agreeable shade to the inmates, who sit upon a low bank or seat of earth, which is made to run along the whole of the walls inside the square. This low bank and the floors, being rubbed over with a wash of red earth, which takes on a fine glaze when dry, and the walls above whitewashed, the whole arrangements have a clean, tidy, and somewhat showy appearance, the picturesque look of which is still farther enhanced by a display of muskets and other warlike accoutrements upon the walls of the principal open apartment, which is used by the master of the establishment as his reception-room and hall of audience.

In other parts of the house we find, suspended from, or nailed to the walls, a variety of portraits and prints, chiefly French, and vile daubs. Africans are exceedingly fond of pictures in their rooms, and to gratify this taste press anything into their service that comes readiest to hand. Napoleon in his cocked hat, in gaudy colours or simple woodcut, on foot and on horseback, and George IV. in his coronation robes, may be seen disputing for space with Punch and his dog Toby, as they appear in the frontispiece of his publication, with the urns, tea and coffee-pots of Cox, Savory, and Company, as seen in their advertisements, or with the royal arms of England flaming in all the glory of an announcement of one of her Majesty's tradesmen.

The introduction of pictures is far from being the only European innovation which attracts our attention. Until inoculated with the fancy for change, which their intercourse with Europeans is daily developing, their household wants were extremely few and of the most simple kind, and with many people in the country, even yet little change has taken place. With a cloth to cover himself, a mat to sleep upon, a few earthen pots for holding water and cooking, a calabash to drink from, a couple of stones to grind his corn, a tub to pound his plantains in, and a bill-hook and hoe to clear his plantation, the Fantee is in a condition to commence housekeeping, with everything necessary for his establishment. Gradually, however, are gathered around him the superfluous luxuries which travel in the wake of the white man. It is amusing to observe, in many of the family houses, the progress of ideas among its inmates, and the various degrees of advancement which they have made, from their different arrangements. Their superstition may be seen in the bottle or string suspended over the doorway, in the Fetish tree in the yard, and in the posts erected in the corners and behind the doors, to sustain vessels which hold Fetish substances.

The old people care not to vary the practice of their fathers, and confine themselves to the simple necessaries of life, not so much that they do not prefer the comforts of more civilized habits, as that they cannot give themselves the trouble to acquire the means to gratify them. The bare clay walls of their apartment, with their mats and stools, their earthen pots and calabashes, bespeak the stagnant nature of their ideas. In another apartment of the same house, we find perhaps dishes of pewter and earthenware, a spoon, a knife and fork, a table, a chair, a bed, and a trunk; and the walls whitewashed, with pictures and the owner's musket and cartouch-box hung upon them. Again we may find, still in the same house, a well-finished room according to our European ideas of comfort, and its inmate dressed like an Englishman, able to read and to write, and having the Bible, Bunyan's " Pilgrim's Progress," and other religious books upon his table or sofa.

This strange intermixture gives a grotesque and comical appearance to their whole arrangements. There are few houses now, however, in the neighbourhood of Cape Coast, and other principal towns, in which many of the comforts and luxuries of civilized life are not to be found ; and many of the natives enjoy a degree of easy abundance, and of luxurious enjoyment, which, until intercourse with them has made it familiar to us, we should not be inclined to associate with the naked simplicity of their attire ; for it is not among those alone who follow European habits of dress that we find all the conveniences of life.

Indeed, among all classes there is a much more general diffusion of a moderate and competent means of subsistence than is to be perhaps found in any other country in the world, absolute want being perfectly unknown. The tendency, however, at present is strong towards a higher standard of excellence in the objects of their pursuit, which are chiefly based upon an anxious desire to imitate European habits of life, which would appear, especially in external acquirements, to be the grand desideratum of young Africa. So great is the competition `in this respect, that it is leading many to ruin; for, not satisfied to wait the slow process of obtaining the means of adding to their enjoyments by habits of frugal industry, by which the road to wealth is open to all, they are apt to launch into extravagant expenses, without at all reflecting upon their capability of supporting them. In this way, it is not at all uncommon to see a person run headlong and deeply into debt, all the while that he is building a house, which may possibly be sold by his creditors even before the projector has managed to make it habitable. Others, with equal imprudence, expend the whole of their means in raising a costly building, which remains a mere unfinished shell—a monument of the folly and of the pride of its owner. Some even make a greater miscalculation of their means than this, and commence a structure upon a scale so disproportioned to their means, that they are compelled to leave it half-finished, to be battered to the ground by the rains. But on all hands we see pretensions to a much higher class of building than the preceding generation considered necessary for their wants, and failure is by no means the invariable result of these ambitious views; on the contrary, there are now to be found many whose houses and mode of life correspond in every respect with our European ideas.

From these remarks, the reader will have little difficulty in picturing to himself the endless variety of degree in the progress made towards the habits of a higher degree of civilization. He will also easily imagine the strange incongruities to be encountered in his researches into the present condition of the people ; for he will look in vain in an African establishment for that nice adjustment and appropriate suitability, which is expressed by being " in keeping," and which is justly considered an indication of correct taste.

The virtue of hospitality is general, and appears so natural to the Fantees, that one of themselves, a stranger, seems to think he has a right to put it to the proof by taking up his temporary abode wherever he thinks fit. Accommodation is readily granted without any expectation of recompense ; and upon occasions of a visit between friends, the guest is invariably received with presents. To Europeans they are so very accommodating, that they do not hesitate to vacate their own houses for a time, in order that they may be properly lodged ; and although they do not provide them with an entertainment which they doubt their ability of making suitable for them, yet do they bring presents of sheep, fowls, yams, plantains and palm-wine, in order that their own servants may prepare the feast. The writer has seen the greatest delicacy evinced in the unobtrusive manner in which real kindnesses have been done; and has himself, during a long residence among them, received so many proofs of their respect and attachment as will ever lead him to regard them with an affectionate and grateful remembrance.

CHAPTER XI

Persecution of the Christians at Assafa—Their offensive conduct — Sacred grove violated—Indignation of the Fetishmen — Council of chiefs—Denunciation of the Fetish worship by a Fetish priest—Destruction of the Christians' village by Adoo, chief of Mankassim — Captivity of the Christians—Interference of the English authorities—Palaver held at Anamaboe—Resistance— Necessity for caution on the part of the authorities— Little dependence to be placed on native co-operation— Meeting with the head men of Cape Coast—Deputation to Adoo—He consults his Fetish, and receives permission to go to Cape Coast—His arrival—Interest felt in his trial—Conspiracy of Fetishmen to poison four supporters of Christianity—Exposure of Fetish tricks—Indignation of the chiefs—They pronounce the Fetishmen worthy of death — Helpless condition of the people bereft of spiritual aid—Their conflicting feelings on the subject.

SINCE writing the chapter upon the Fetish worship of the people, in which we represented the struggle going on between the two great principles of barbarism and civilization, the views which we then expressed have received an extraordinary corroboration from circumstances which have since taken place. At the small village of Assafa, which is not far distant from the great Braffo Fetish of Mankassim, Mr. Freeman had established a school and admitted to Christian fellowship a small body of adult converts to Christianity. It was a cause of great indignation to the Fetishmen to see their worship repudiated in the immediate vicinity of the chief Fetish of the country, and they commenced a series of annoying persecutions, by which they hoped to extinguish the spirit of Fetish repudiation. To escape from these annoyances, the Christian converts removed from Assafa, and established themselves in a small village under their head man " Old Quashie," who had renounced Fetish. This removal only brought them nearer to the Fetish grove, and exposed them still more to the vengeance of the Fetishmen. Nor was the conduct of these proselytes at all times calculated to avoid giving offence. They appeared to believe that the best way of displaying their zeal for Christianity, was to insult the worshippers of Fetish, and they took no pains to conceal their detestation, which they expressed by making a mock of their worship, and by a general abuse of the worshippers.

Moreover they cleared the bush and made their

plantation in the immediate vicinity of the sacred grove, which they approached with a levity and irreverence highly displeasing to the Fetishmen, who urged upon the Fantee chiefs the necessity of avenging their insulted god. The believers in Fetish generally, however, did not consider their interference necessary, as they had great faith in the power of their chief deity to avenge himself, and they believed that he would be induced to make some signal demonstration of his wrath against the profane contemners of his power. Their faith in this hope was, however, disappointed, for the plantations which they thought must be blighted were particularly fruitful, and a still more marked indignity failed to rouse the anger of the god. One of the Christian converts did not fear to shoot a deer within the precincts of the grove, which was regarded as such a flagrant contempt of the great Fetish, that the priest at last prevailed upon the Fantee chiefs to take the matter into their serious consideration. A council was held, at which it was agreed that the chiefs would mutually support each other in punishing the next insult offered to their deity. Adoo, the chief of Mankassim, (the representative of the former kings of Fantee, when the nation acknowledged one king,) was appointed guardian of the Fetish. The other chiefs promised him their support, and consented to share the responsibility of any measure which he might find it necessary to adopt in reference to the charge imposed upon him.

Affairs were in this state, when a Fetishman—one who had been an inferior servitor at the altar of the great Fetish—renounced his worship and joined the other converts to Christianity. This defection still farther alarmed the Fetishmen, and they only watched for an opportunity to cut him off. He soon afforded them one, for he was influenced by the rancour of a renegade against his old associates, and spared no pains to evince his contempt for them. Actuated by this spirit, he and two others ventured to cut some sticks within the grove; which the Fetishmen no sooner heard, than they had recourse to Adoo to punish the offenders. This chief, burning with a fiery zeal in the cause of the Fetish, and relying upon the support of the other Fantee chiefs, immediately summoned his retainers, and set out for Old Quashie's village, where the delinquents resided. He arrived at daybreak, before the villagers had risen from their beds. He seized and bound the Christians, and carried them captive to Mankassim, leaving their houses in flames.

Information of this outrage was conveyed to the judicial assessor in a letter written by one of the educated natives in the neighbourhood. Until the receipt of this communication, the English authorities had no knowledge whatever of the council of the chiefs, or of the other circumstances connected with this affair. A soldier was immediately sent to Mankassim to demand the liberation of the prisoners, and to cite Adoo to appear at Cape Coast Castle, to explain and account for his conduct. At the same time, the assessor, persuaded that such a gross violation of authority, the like of which had not occurred since the close of the Ashantee war, could only have been committed by a man who had made up his mind to dare the worst, privately requested Ammooney, the chief of Anamaboe, to use his influence with Adoo to induce him to submit to the authorities and to obey the summons.

In the meantime the Fetishmen were instigating him to drown the renegade, by the terrors of the offended deity and every inducement which they could think of, but he trembled to take this decisive step. He still respected the English government, and he refused to commit an act which he could not help regarding as an entire renunciation of his allegiance. While this debate was going on, the summons reached him, which being supported by Ammooney's strong persuasions, had the effect of recalling him to a sense of his danger. He consented to appear at Cape Coast upon a day mentioned, excusing himself from accompanying the soldier, upon the plea that he could not collect his retainers, who must follow him, under the delay of a few days. He promised that he would bring his prisoners with him, and that no injury should befal them. This answer not being satisfactory, another messenger was sent to him demanding his immediate obedience to the summons. By this time, however, he was ready to come, the whole of the Fantee chiefs having espoused his cause as that of the Fetish, and prepared themselves to accompany him, and to support him by their countenance at his trial. When they arrived at Anamaboe they wrote a letter to Mr. Bannerman, the governor, praying him not to insist upon their coming to Cape Coast, as they had a great many followers with them, whom they would find it difficult to support there, and entreating him to send the assessor to Anamaboe " to hear the palaver," giving at the same time the strongest assurances that they would entirely abide by his decision.

Their request was granted, and the case was investigated at Anamaboe ; but the assessor was not a little astonished to find, on landing upon the beach there, that the whole of the Fantee chiefs, with fully three thousand followers, were congregated to watch the proceedings. He found the facts of the case to be what we have here stated. It was evident, by their own admission, as well as by the testimony of others, that the Christian converts had intentionally insulted the worshippers of the Fetish, and their conduct had been calculated with a view to provoke them. Nor did Adoo seek to deny his act, which he and his brother chiefs justified as a duty which he owed to his gods. The merits of the case were, therefore, easily comprehended ; but it was not so easy to decide upon the best manner of treating it. There was a necessity for the calmest deliberation, for a due allowance being made for the prejudices of the people, who had faith in their Fetish, and for the exhibition of the most impartial consideration, without regard for Christian or heathen. It was decided that Adoo should pay to the Christians the full value of the property destroyed by the burning of their huts, which was calculated at £56, and that, moreover, he should pay a fine of £40 to her Majesty for his flagrant contempt of the law. The insulters of the Fetish were adjudged to pay £20 to the Fantee chiefs, as compensation for the insults offered them through their Fetish. It may perhaps be thought that the treatment they had received, had been sufficient to relieve them from further punishment, and that the lawlessness of Adoo's act had forfeited every title to a consideration of their insulted feelings. But without basing the whole decision upon the original merits of the case, it would have been impossible to convince the Fetish worshippers that favour and partiality had not keen shown to the Christians; for in dealing out justice to them, it is more necessary to mark, by comparative penalties, our sense of the different degrees of culpability, than, after carefully summing up the evidence, to strike the balance of guiltiness and affix a single penalty upon the greatest offender.

The circumstances of important cases are extensively, although often imperfectly, known to the public; and it is only by the amount of penalty that they can estimate the Europeans' views of justice, as the strictures of the judge are not generally heard. As soon as judgment was given in this case, the chiefs requested, as they often do, to be allowed to retire for a few minutes to consult upon it. When they returned to the hall, they acknowledged its justice in respect to the compensation decreed for themselves, and the fine imposed for the violation of the law, and expressed their perfect readiness to abide by the decision to this extent; but their whole sentiments revolted against the idea of compensating the Christians for their losses. These were, in their eyes, altogether an inadequate punishment for the affronts offered to the Fetish. They, therefore, argued strenuously against submission upon this point, and alleged that they could not compromise the dignity of the great

Fetish by yielding to a payment which must greatly offend their god. They, moreover, insisted that the Christians should be prevented from returning to their village and plantations as a mark of deference to the Fetish, essential to avert his wrath from the whole country.

Their arguments were met by a firm assertion of the principles of justice, which could not be allowed to truckle to their prejudices. They were given to understand that the local government had established, and were determined to maintain, security and protection for all; not even injustice arising from their Fetish partialities could be allowed to form an exception to this rule. Care was taken to explain to them that the conduct of the Christians was disapproved of, and that while the prejudices of the people led them to reverence their Fetish groves, the magistrates would regard their wilful desecration in the same light, in performing justice between man and man, as they would the spoliation of a missionary chapel. The fine imposed upon the Christians was an evidence of this impartial view of the case. Such insults were neither dictated by a Christian spirit, nor calculated to recommend Christianity to others. It was perfectly possible for Christians and Fetish worshippers to live together in the same country, without mutually offending each other.

While the assessor insisted upon compensation being made for the losses sustained, and thus justified and explained the grounds of his decision, and the principles upon which he acted, he, at the same time, expressed his willingness to mediate between them, in order to remove occasions of future quarrels. With this view, although he would neither compel nor sanction the abandonment of their plantations, merely to gratify the superstitious feelings of the Fetish worshippers, yet he would recommend the Christians to sell them; and if the chiefs were sincere in their desire to do honour to their Fetish, they would not object to make some sacrifice, to preserve the inviolability of his abode.

Although these arguments were neither satisfactory nor convincing—for the assessor was reasoning with them upon the only subject on which they will not listen to reason—yet they established in the minds of the chiefs and people the conviction that the government was pursuing in this matter the same system of impartial justice which they had observed to characterise its general conduct. They had the penetration to perceive the inutility of attempting to alter this policy, and they sorrowfully submitted themselves to the decision, saying: "If our master prefers these ten Christians to the whole of the Fantee nation, we cannot help it; we are sorry, but we submit."

In this remark we have an excellent illustration of their ideas of justice. It would never occur to them to support a principle, in opposition to such a numerical opposition. It implied also a partial disruption of the cordial ties which had hitherto united them to the government, their great attachment to their Fetish rendering their present submission a severe struggle between the duty required of them by their faith, and that imposed upon them by a government which they loved and respected, and of whose power to benefit them they were fully conscious. Seeing no means of overcoming the assessor's determination, Ottoo, chief of Abrah, and Ammooney, chief of Anamaboe, became responsible for the payment of the fine and compensation-money on the morrow. Then they left the fort, much dejected at the result of the investigation.

It had been necessary to close the gates of the fort, to exclude the retainers of the chiefs, who were anxious to be present. About two hundred of the principal men were all that the hall could accommodate. The others took up a position outside the gate, and waited with much impatience the result of the trial. As soon as it was announced to them, they flew to their arms, which had been deposited in the houses of their Anamaboe friends, and in less than ten minutes Adoo was surrounded by fully a thousand of adherents, who raised him upon their heads, and carried him in defiant triumph through the town. It appeared that these measures had all been previously arranged by a party of the bush chiefs, without the connivance or knowledge of the Anamaboes and Abrahs. Their object in obtaining a hearing of the palaver at Anamaboe, instead of Cape Coast, had been to be out of reach of physical coercion, which the presence of troops in garrison there afforded. They believed it possible to awe the assessor, unsupported as he was by any present protection, into a compliance with their wishes in the settlement of the case. Failing in this, they had resolved to withstand his authority, and to brave his displeasure, and the manner in which they now acted but too plainly evinced their feelings.

While they paraded Adoo through the streets, they sung the praises of the Fetish, proclaimed the merits of the chief as its protecting hero, and heaped insult and abuse upon the Christians and their aiders and abettors. A few kegs of powder were carried before Adoo during this progress, to intimate that he was prepared to fight in defence of his gods. An occasional shout to slay and exterminate the Christians, was sometimes made. The assessor, fearing that they might proceed to extremities, and having great reliance on his influence over them, which had on many previous occasions been successfully employed in like tumultuous uproars, determined to go out and endeavour to disperse them. He proceeded directly to that part of the procession where Adoo was elevated on the heads of his bearers. He indignantly ordered him to descend and dismiss his attendants. He came down from his palanquin accordingly; but his retainers, thinking that the assessor's object was to take him prisoner, hurried him off in another direction.

By this time many of the Anamaboes, getting alarmed for the white man's safety, hastened to his protection, and ranging themselves around him with heavy sticks and cutlasses in their hands, were eager to come to blows with the bush people, who seeing the turn which matters were taking, became alarmed, and took to flight in the direction of their homes. In two minutes there was not one of them to be seen in Anamaboe. Nor did they slacken their flight until they had put some miles between them and the town.

As soon as Ammooney heard that Adoo had left the town, he began to have an unpleasant sense of his responsibility for the payment of the sums which had been decreed. He therefore hastened after him, to endeavour to persuade him to return without his followers, and to wait the final settlement of the palaver. He came up with him at Great Cormantine, but he could make no impression upon him of the kind which he desired. On the contrary, Adoo reviled him and Ottoo as traitors to the Fetish, and to the covenant which they had made together to defend their common worship. He told him that he had only come to Anamaboe to have the case heard, in the confidence that the Fantees were all so firmly leagued together on this point, that the white men would not dare to punish him. But he had found them submissive in everything to the assessor, and he now meant to leave them to make good the liability which they had undertaken. Ammooney returned home disconsolate, amidst the jeers and execrations of the women in the villages through which he passed, who were all on the side of the Fetish hero.

Many subsequent attempts were made to induce Adoo to submit to the authorities, and to come to the castle; but he equally disregarded the summons of the governor, and the persuasions of many of his countrymen. He provided himself with powder and lead, cut war-paths through the bush, and maintained himself for four months in an attitude of armed defiance. He was supported in his resistance by many of the Fantee chiefs, who, assembling in the neighbourhood of the Fetish grove, kept watch and ward lest any sudden attempt should be made to seize Adoo, or to destroy the sacred abode. During this time, the more favourably-disposed chiefs endeavoured to mediate between him and the governor, and were willing to pay the fine. The amount decreed to compensate the losses of the Christians was still a stumbling-block for all, although Ammooney and Ottoo did not refuse to redeem their responsibility. A half-way submission of this kind was deemed unsatisfactory, and the authorities preferred to wait the progress of events, rightly judging that the state of uncertainty in which Adoo and his friends were, and the interruption which his hostile attitude was giving to commercial intercourse, would soon become intolerable to all parties, and render them sincerely desirous of a settlement. It was also prudent not to aggravate the feelings of the people on the subject of their Fetish.

Adoo's was a holy warfare, and the sympathies of the masses were on his side. There would have been difficulty in knowing whom to trust in such an emergency. It was not like the Appollonian campaign, in which every one was anxious to take a part. Their superstitious fears would have paralyzed the courage of native auxiliaries, if a sense of religious duty might not even have rendered them treacherous allies. Under these circumstances, it was necessary for the governor to observe the greatest caution and circumspection; and it was only when murmurs of discontent throughout the country became general and loud, and the natives were made fully sensible of the necessity of bringing Adoo to obedience, that vigorous measures were resolved upon.

The king and head men of Cape Coast were summoned to attend the governor and council in the castle, and being informed that it was the intention of the governor to send an expeditionary force against 'Adoo, were asked if they would give their assistance. This question occasioned a good deal of hesitation, and they retired to consult before they would venture to give a decided answer. On their return, they acknowledged Adoo's conduct to be very bad, and also the necessity of reducing him to obedience ; but they did not see how they could go and fight against the Braffo Fetish. It was true, the Cape Coast people were the soldiers of the fort, and were ready, on all ordinary occasions, to fight the battles of their English masters ; but the governor must make allowances for them, if they hesitated to engage in a war which so deeply implicated the religious feelings of the whole people. They begged that he would defer his intention of proceeding to hostilities for a week, to allow them to send a fresh deputation to Adoo and the people with him ; hoping by their persuasions to influence him to submit. If their remonstrances should prove ineffectual, they would no longer withhold their assistance, as they were convinced of the necessity of supporting the authority of the government. The governor gladly accepted this conditional promise of their co-operation, and to give weight to the representations of the deputation, active and ostentatious preparations were made for war, in order that the public rumour of them might intimidate the recusant chief. The soldiers were daily paraded and exercised at target practice, and trained to the use of the rocket-guns and field-pieces, and other indications given of the earnest intentions of the governor. The deputation, before leaving, were anxious to receive assurances that Adoo would not be imprisoned, but the governor disdained to give any pledge of the kind. The submission, if made at all, must be full and entire. The insubordinate opposition of Adoo and his abettors at length gave way before these moving arguments. He accompanied the deputation to Cape Coast, attended by most of the Fantee chiefs, with a very numerous retinue of armed followers. A bold attempt was made to induce the governor to consent to have the palaver heard outside the castle, upon the plea that there was no room sufficient to contain such a numerous assembly. This concession was firmly denied, and Adoo was compelled to humble himself, and to submit to such terms as the governor chose to grant him.

Upon the day appointed for receiving Adoo's submission, Cape Coast presented a scene of extraordinary bustle and excitement. All the streets and thoroughfares were thronged with crowds of eager groups talking over the great event of the day, and speculating upon its probable termination. Some latent hopes still lurked in the minds of the Fetish worshippers, that the governor would be deterred by the display of their great numbers, from proceeding to extremities against Adoo; but if they ever contemplated farther resistance, their hopes of success must have been entirely destroyed by the precautionary measures which were taken to maintain the peace of the town. An officer and a party of gunners were stationed in Fort William Tower, which completely commands the castle, the town, and its approaches. The soldiers in the garrison were under arms. The gates were closed, and only a small wicket left open for the admission of the chiefs. The sentries were doubled, and the officer in charge of the gate had orders to admit only the principal men. By ten o'clock they began to arrive, and to take up their seats in the largest hall of the castle. It was nearly twelve before Adoo made his appearance, escorted by the Cape Coast deputation. He entered the castle with great state and show, and seemed offended that his drummers and horn-blower were not allowed to attend him. He was dressed in a very rich yellow silk damask cloth. His wrists and ankles were profusely decorated with golden ornaments, while a string of valuable beads, interspersed with lumps of rock-gold encircled his neck, and hung down upon his breast. His air was altogether a strange mixture of stately dignity, blustering swagger, and stealthy apprehension. While his

pompous walk and assumed unconcern revealed his
sense of the consequence attached to his position
on such an occasion, the quick furtive glances of
his unsteady eye, as it rested for an instant upon
the small groups of soldiers sauntering in the yard,
and the lowering scowl of his bloated face, betrayed
the uneasiness of his mind. The traces of a long
debauch were strongly marked on his countenance,
giving evidence that he had been seeking relief
from his fears in sensual indulgence during his prolonged contumacy. He was preceded by several
sword-bearers, carrying his large gold-handled
swords of state, and his linguist, with his silverheaded cane of office, and was followed by an
attendant with the royal stool and cushion.

As soon as he had taken his seat in the great
palaver hall, the governor received notice that the
chiefs were prepared to see him. He accordingly
proceeded to join the assembly, accompanied by his
council, the magistrates, and several of the military
officers of the garrison. When they had taken
their seats at the farther end of the room, and
had leisure to observe the whole appearance and
arrangements of this large congress, it was impossible to avoid being much struck with the strange
character of the scene. Fully six hundred of the
principal men of the country were assembled within

the hall. They were seated on chairs and country stools along the walls, and on to the centre of the wide floor, through which a small clear passage, to admit of ingress or egress to the governor's seat, was the only space left unoccupied. The rest was one dense mass of living men, so closely packed together, that not a vestige of the floor was visible. The great irregularity in the height of their seats, some being on high chairs, others on stools of all sizes, and the sprinkling of attendants who had been admitted, squatted on the bare floor, still farther added to the grotesque appearance of the assembly; while the rich and variegated colours of their robes, contrasting with the darkness of their skins, the sheen of gold and silver which glittered on many of their persons, the gold-handled swords of state, which marked the position of some principal chief, the switching of the elephants' tails by the little pages, and the monkey skull-caps of the chiefs' court-criers gave additional variety to the scene. Add to these the grave deportment of the head men, with their long dark or grizzled beards, the eager upturned gaze of all eyes in the direction of the white men, the solemn and dignified bearing of the governor and magistrates, the presence of a minister of the Christian religion, with a band of native converts deeply interested in

the result of the question, and behind all the martial
figures and bold mien of gallant English officers,
in full military equipments, and the reader has
before him a combination of features, which, taken
in connexion with the high moral and religious considerations involved in the struggle, must deeply
impress him with the strange interest of the scene.

Great formality is observed by the Fantees upon
occasions of this description. The business was
opened by the Cape Coast deputation coming up
to the governor's table, and relating through their
linguist, the whole proceedings, from the time that
the governor had asked their assistance, until
their arrival with Adoo on the floor of the hall.
Having finished their narration, they turned round
to this chief, and leading him to the governor's
chair, retired to their seats. Adoo made a deep
obeisance to his excellency, throwing his handker-
chief at his feet, to indicate the humble and submissive position in which he placed himself. He
then bowed consecutively to the magistrates and
officers, and drew himself up in an attitude of
respectful attention before the governor.

Being required to explain his conduct, he
acknowledged his error, and craved mercy. He
did not regard the question much as his own,
as that of the whole Fantee nation, and he acted

in defence of his Fetish, on the strength of a covenant which he had made with his brother chiefs. He was very wrong in having so long resisted the governor's summons, but he was afraid of the assessor, whom he regarded as his personal enemy, as he had, on several previous occasions, severly punished him. He protested against the judgment he had given in the present case, and prayed the governor and magistrates, in conjunction with the Fantee chiefs, to give it a rehearing, declaring himself perfectly willing to abide by their decision. The assessor was quite willing that his decision should be set aside, and had no fears of submitting his judgment to the impartial consideration of the present assembly. The same evidence was gone over which had been adduced at Anamaboe, and when the investigation was finished, the governor, magistrates, and principal chiefs, retired to consult upon it, without the assessor.

On their return to the hall, it was announced to Adoo that they fully concurred in the decision which had been given at Anamaboe, and that he must now submit to the payment of the sums decreed by the assessor. The governor, in consideration of the entreaties of the other chiefs, and being satisfied that his authority had been fully vindicated without any unworthy compromise, consented to forgive Adoo for his contumacy, and not to inflict any additional punishment upon him. He insisted, however, on his depositing a security of fifty ounces of gold-dust in the castle, as a pledge that he would observe a perfect obedience for the space of two years. The fine and the compensation to the Christians having been paid, this troublesome question was finally set at rest.

But the effects of this religious excitement were not confined to the case in question. During these four months of antagonism, the minds of men had been directed to their system of Fetish worship with a more intelligent and reasoning scrutiny, than they had ever before exercised. The defection of several of the priests, and the disclosures which they did not hesitate to make of the tricks of the Fetishmen, had a tendency to weaken the confidence of the natives generally. Several of the chiefs, who had hitherto been blind followers of the Fetishmen, were anxious that the white men should institute an inquiry into their proceedings, evidently prepared, if the investigation should prove their pretensions to be founded on lies and cheats, to throw off their grievous yoke.

The consequence of this infidel spirit was a

more determined and concentrated effort on the part of the Fetishmen to prop up their tottering power. This feeling, more than the insults of the Assafa Christians, was the occasion of the council of Fantee chiefs upon the subject, and of Adoo's outrageous act. They had observed, with a bitter hate, the prevalence of new ideas destructive of their authority, and while they had yet influence over the superstitious fears of the people, they instigated the Fantee chiefs to make an united effort to maintain the supremacy of the Fetish. It was also the persuasions of the Fetishmen, founded upon pretended communications with the great Fetish, that kept Adoo so long firm in his recusancy. He was confirmed in the course which they had compelled him to adopt by frequent messages from the deity.

The Fetishmen were daily inquiring of their god, what was to be the result of the struggle, and the responses which they pretended to receive buoyed up Adoo with a superstitious confidence. Upon the receipt of the governor's summons, he never manifested the smallest disrespect. On the contrary, he always acknowledged the English as his masters, whom he was ready to obey, and expressed his willingness to proceed to Cape Coast, provided the Fetish would give him permission.

He invariably went up to inquire of the god, before he presumed to give an answer, and his repeated refusals were couched in the most respectful terms. Even when the Cape Coast deputation went to him, he did not deviate from this course. He received the members of it with much kindness and hospitality, and asked them to remain a few days until he could receive an answer from the Fetish. He made sacrifices and inquired, and on this occasion was answered that he might go without fear. Many circumstances combined to influence the Fetishmen to hold out no longer.

In the earlier stages of the contention, they had hoped to be able to constrain the Fetish worshippers to rise as one man to assert Fetish supremacy ; but the defection of the chiefs of Anamaboe and Abrah, gave alarming token of their waning power. They did not, however, despair of being able to recal them to their worship, and they continued sending them threatening messages from their god, with the view of effecting this purpose. They seized upon every untoward circumstance which occurred, and attributed it to the wrath of the great Fetish. No rain had fallen during these months, the country was parched with drought, and the people suffered from a deficiency of water. This, of course, was the work of the Fetish, a demonstration of his anger, which was not without its effect upon the minds of the natives generally.

During the investigation at Anamaboe, Ottoo, the chief of Abrah, fell down in a faint in the hall of the fort, and died about two months afterwards, while the excitement was still going on. This was a still more signal mark of the vengeance of the Fetish, as he was a firm supporter of English authority. We are not altogether without suspicions, that his death ought to be attributed to the agency of the Fetishmen. At all events, the sequel will show that they were very capable of dealing with poison. Mr. George Blankson, a native merchant in Anamaboe, Mr. Hayfron, the fort interpreter, and Mr. William Parker and Mr. Stanhope, office-bearers of the Wesleyan church, and strong supporters of Christian religion, had rendered themselves particularly obnoxious on account of the active part which they were taking in these proceedings. The Fetishmen believed, if they could manage to cut these men off, that it would not be difficult to persuade their superstitious dupes that the great Fetish had killed them. With this view, a council of Fetishmen and Fetish-women was held in the dead of night, in a lonely spot on the margin of a small salt lake, near Anamaboe.

Here they concerted their diabolical plans, and bound themselves by a great oath to secrecy. A subscription was made for the purpose of engaging the services of some Fetishman, skilled in poison, who was to be hired to put them to death. While they were thus making their preparations to establish anew the authority of the great Fetish by such unscrupulous measures, the growing discontent of the people, and the active preparations of the governor, alarmed many of the Anamaboe Fetishmen, who urged upon the Braffo priests the necessity of allowing Adoo to go to Cape Coast, and of trusting to the chapter of accidents for the re-establishment of their authority. Many of them saw that their brethren at Mankassin had overshot the mark, by counselling Adoo's continued resistance, and they trembled for the entire overthrow of their power by a longer persistence.

The whole of the Fetish priests during this time, were in a state of great excitement. Their entire crafty system, by which they obtained a means of livelihood, was in danger. Some of them, perceiving it to be a falling cause, were anxious to separate themselves in time from their community, and thus to escape the punishment which seemed inevitable, while others pressed upon he priests of the great Fetish the necessity of lowering their pretensions, if they would not consent to see the whole of their privileges overthrown.

These circumstances were privately communicated to the assessor, about the time of Adoo's arrival at Cape Coast, by one of the Fetishmen, named Cofee Coomah, who had been present at the unholy council near the salt pond at Anamaboe. He gave him a list of the men and women who had been present upon this occasion, and provided him with sufficient proofs of their guilt. He moreover disclosed the whole clap-trap of the Braffo Fetishmen, their practice of stationing their accomplices in the leafy recesses of the sacred grove, to utter in an unnatural voice the oracles of the god, and of placing others among the branches of the trees over the heads of the supplicants to receive the offerings which they presented with downcast eyes and with their hands extended to the heavens, and which they believed to be taken up by the god.

The assessor's informant had no personal knowledge of these facts, nor until lately had it ever occurred to him that the Braffo Fetish was not possessed of supernatural power. He acknowledged that he had himself, as a Fetishman, practised tricks to deceive his dupes, but his fearful respect for the great Fetish would not allow him to believe that the Braffo priests had recourse to a system of trick and deception. The circumstance which led to his conviction upon this point, arose out of the violation of his wife by a brother Fetishman. The woman, who had gone to consult this Fetishman respecting the sickness of a child, had been compelled to submit to the embraces of the priest. She informed her husband, who went to expostulate with the ravisher. The latter accused the woman of speaking falsely, and asserted his innocence.

Upon this, Cofee Coomah insisted that they should both go to the great Fetish, and learn the truth from the Braffo priests. Whereupon he was told that the great Fetish was no god, that the Fetishmen there were as great rogues as themselves, that they only cheated the people with tricks, and that he himself had frequently been employed to assist them, and had often pronounced the oracles which had previously been agreed upon by the priests. He mentioned the name of this man and several others, as persons who could reveal the whole system of deception.

With the knowledge of these facts, the assessor determined to expose the Fetishmen to the whole of the people; and when Adoo's affair was settled,

he startled the assembly by announcing that he
had now the intention of showing them what kind
of people they had been supporting, almost to the
verge of bringing utter destruction upon the
country.   He charged the Fetishmen with a conspiracy to commit murder, and stated that he had
proofs to lay before them of their guilt, as well as
of the gross deceptions which they practised, and
he invited them to appear in the castle on the
morrow to be present at this investigation.

This announcement was received by the chiefs
with a variety of emotions.   Some of them,
staunch supporters of the Fetish, shrank from an
exposure of the kind ; and others, and especially the
Abrahs and Anamaboes, whose faith was greatly
shaken, were anxious to have their doubts resolved,
and their consciences eased by the conviction of
the Fetish impostures.   The chiefs were ordered
to bring the Fetishmen of their several districts
into court, and the predominant desire to have the
matter thoroughly sifted was evidenced by the
alacrity with which they sent for them.   Adoo's
case had sunk into perfect insignificance, before
the weightier considerations involved in the present
accusations.

With reference to this point, it is sufficient to
state that the conspiracy to poison was fully proved

and acknowledged by the Fetishmen themselves. Nineteen of them, men and women, were fully convicted of this heinous crime, and the assessor had the satisfaction of gaining over the chiefs to their punishment. They were even willing to outvie him in severity, and pronounced the criminals worthy of death. The men were sentenced to be publicly flogged, and to be imprisoned and put to hard labour for the space of five years. The women, in consideration of their sex, got off with two years imprisonment. The public whipping of the dreaded Fetishmen was inflicted in the market-place of Cape Coast, amidst the universal applause of the people.

Upon the subject of the Fetishmen's tricks and deceptions, no less curiosity was evinced. The exposure of these struck at the very root of their faith, and an eagerness proportioned to its importance was accordingly felt. For three long days during which the investigation took place, the large hall was as crowded as on the first day of Adoo's trial ; and when conviction was at last clearly brought home to the minds of the people, it was curious to observe its effect upon different minds. Some rejoiced, some grieved, some laughed, and some were indignant. Several of the Fetishmen's accomplices, who had been employed to speak the oracles, revealed their whole proceedings, and gave proofs of the truth of their statements, by mentioning the occasions on which they had answered the supplicants, many of whom were present.

Then might be seen an angry chief press forward, to abuse these luckless accomplices, with such taunts as these, " Were you the god that pronounced me guilty of perjury ?" " Was it you that made me pay my money in vain to cure my child's sickness ?" " Did you fix upon me the guilt of witchcraft ?" And as they lashed themselves into a passion, with the thought of the tricks which had been played upon them, they threatened the culprits with vengeance and restitution. No one was more enraged than Adoo. Here was before him the self-acknowledged god, who had prevented him from obeying the governor's summons, fully revealed in the very shabby person of one of his own vassals. He taunted him with all the sufferings which he had caused him to endure, and actually wept at the bare imagination of his folly.

One venerable chief, when order was somewhat restored, rose, and pointing to his long white beard, said : " This teaches me that I am too old to learn ; but it ought to give weight to the advice which I now give to all who are young, to give up their Fetish and to go to school." It was impossible to see their only stay and support, thus rudely shattered to pieces, without a feeling of pity for their desolate condition, bereft of every spiritual trust. Many of them left the castle sorrowful and downcast, and were heard repeating to each other, " What can we now do in sickness and distress ?" " Whither can we fly for succour ?" " Our gods have been proved to be no gods !" " Our priests have deceived us !"

When the writer left the coast, the altar of the great Fetish, who had been reverently worshipped for ages, was entirely deserted, and the sacred persons of the priests were no longer of any account. Adoo, attributing his losses and misfortunes to them, had compelled them to refund the money which had been taken from him.

It is not intended to convey the impression, that the conviction of the roguery of this, the principal Fetish of the country, has eradicated the desire to worship Fetishes. This desire will remain, until their minds have become enlightened by a knowledge of the Christian religion, for the introduction of which, this sapping of their former faith has clearly paved the way. It speaks well for the docile disposition of the people, that such a movement has been effected without bloodshed. At one time our power and influence trembled in the scale, and nothing but the calm and temperate measures of the government prevented a fearful calamity.*

* As this work was about to go to press, the author received a letter from Mr. Freeman, from the Gold Coast, which has been added in an appendix. The reader will perceive that the effects of this exposure have even exceeded the author's expectations.

APPENDIX.

Extract from a Letter of the Rev. T. B. Freeman, dated Cape Coast, September 30, 1852.

" I have long felt desirous to write a few lines, giving you a little information respecting the state of our work here since you left us; but whenever a vessel has been sailing, I have been so hardly pressed with official duties, that I have been compelled to forego that pleasure. I cannot, however, allow this vessel to leave without conveying to you a few lines from me.

" Since your departure from the coast, many deeply interesting circumstances, indicating the growing ascendancy of Christian truth have occurred; and the practical results of the destruction of the pernicious influence of the Grand Fetish are now being clearly developed. The little church at Assafa* now contains upwards of eighty

---

* It was against this small body of Christians that Adoo went in the cause of the Fetish; they then, I believe, numbered fourteen.

members. Fourteen candidates for Christian society have sprung up in a village called Kuntu, about an hour's journey from Assafa. The station at Salt Pond, abandoned some time ago, has been reopened under very promising circumstances.

"Mankassim is to become a mission station in a few days. Winnebah is also to be reoccupied with every prospect of future success. Adoo,* the Chief of Mankassim engages to put fifteen children in the Mankassim school from his own household, and shows the vast change his mind has undergone on the great subject of Christianity, by attending Divine worship in our chapel here, when he comes to Cape Coast. What an extraordinary change! Yamiki, the Chief of Abuadzi, has recently built a nice little chapel entirely at his own expense. Throughout the Abrah country there seems to be a great movement in favour of Christianity. Dominassi, Abuadzi, Dunkwa, Abakrampa and Akroful stations, are all under the happiest influences.

"A short time after your departure for England, we received instructions from our committee in London, to ordain Mr. Martin, our senior native brother, to the full authority and responsibilities of the ministerial office, and the interesting event took place on Monday last, the 27th instant. We had nearly three hundred Christian strangers at Cape Coast to attend the special services connected with the ordination of Mr. Martin.† The chapel was crowded to excess, so much so, that we were obliged to set a watch

* This is the same chief who was so zealous in the Fetish cause; and the new school is established on the ruins of the Grand Fetish.

† This young preacher has been entirely educated in the country, and is a very well-informed man.

at the steps of the gallery, to keep it from being over-filled and broken down. It has been an exhibition of the growing influence of Christianity quite unexampled in this country since the commencement of our mission here, and it has evidently made a deep impression on the public mind.

" Beulah still wears a pleasing aspect. I inclose you a hastily taken copy of my report of it, addressed to the Governor in February last. Perhaps you may be able kindly to make some use of it to our advantage in a pecuniary point of view; there being, I think, many benevolent persons, who though of a different religious persuasion to our own, would readily aid us in such an enterprize as that of Beulah.

" We all hope we shall soon have the pleasure of seeing you safely returned to Cape Coast again to exert your extensive influence in favour of Christian civilization."